THE LAW OF THE EUCHARIST

THE LAW OF THE EUCHARIST

Radbertus vs. Ratramnus
—Their Controversy as to
the Nature of the Eucharist

RELIGION AND LAW SERIES, VOLUME THREE

George J. Gatgounis

WIPF & STOCK · Eugene, Oregon

THE LAW OF THE EUCHARIST
Radbertus vs. Ratramnus—Their Controversy as to the Nature of the Eucharist

Religion and Law Series, Volume Three

Copyright © 2021 George J. Gatgounis. All rights reserved. Except for brief quotations in critical publications or reviews, no part of this book may be reproduced in any manner without prior written permission from the publisher. Write: Permissions, Wipf and Stock Publishers, 199 W. 8th Ave., Suite 3, Eugene, OR 97401.

Wipf & Stock
An Imprint of Wipf and Stock Publishers
199 W. 8th Ave., Suite 3
Eugene, OR 97401

www.wipfandstock.com

PAPERBACK ISBN: 978-1-7252-6122-8
HARDCOVER ISBN: 978-1-7252-6123-5
EBOOK ISBN: 978-1-7252-6124-2

AUGUST 11, 2021

CONTENTS

RADBERTUS AND RATRAMNUS—THEIR CONTROVERSY REGARDING THE EUCHARIST | 1

INTRODUCTION | 3
  Who Were the Carolingians? | 3
    The Carolingians | 3
    Carolingian Academic Disciplines Significant
      to the Eucharistic Controversy | 4
    Who Was Ratramn? | 5
    Who Was Radbert? | 6
  The Eucharistic Controversy Among Other Carolingians | 8
  Scope and Statement of Thesis | 9
    Delimitations | 9
    Statement of Thesis | 10

Chapter 1
THE INTERRELATION OF RADBERT AND RATRAMN ON THE NATURE OF THE EUCHARISTIC ELEMENTS | 11
  Who Is Responding to Whom? | 11
  Common Ground and Point of Divergence | 13

Chapter 2
RADBERT'S VIEW OF THE ELEMENTS IN THE EUCHARIST | 15
  The Nature of the Eucharist | 15

What Is a Sacrament in General? | 15
Radbert's Theology of Transformation—What Happens
    to the Elements? | 17
  The Means of Transformation | 17
  The Nature of the Consecrated Elements | 18
    The Consecrated Elements Actually Transubstantiated | 18
    The Reason the Transubstantiated Elements
        Appear the Same | 21
    The Truth/Figure Distinction in the Elements | 22
  Analogs to the Elements | 22
    The Comparison of New Testament Truth
        and Old Testament Figure | 22
    The Analogy of Baptism | 24
    The Analogy of the Written Word of God | 24
    The Analogy of the Incarnation | 25
    The Analogy of Sacrifice | 25

Chapter 3
THE RESULT OF WORTHY PARTAKING
OF THE ELEMENTS | 27
  Description of the Requisite Worthiness—To Be in Christ | 27
  Description of the Requisite Worthiness—To Partake
      by Faith | 28
  The Result of Unworthy Partaking of the Elements | 29

Chapter 4
RATRAMN'S VIEW OF THE ELEMENTS IN THE EUCHA-
RIST: AN INTRODUCTION TO RATRAMN'S VIEW | 32
  What Are the Issues? | 32
    The Motive and Challenge of Ratramn's Treatise | 32
    The Issue Addressed in Ratramn's Treatise | 33
  Ratramn's Thesis | 33
  Ratramn's Definition of His Terms | 36
    Interpreting Ratramn's Use of the Term "Figure" | 38
  A Précis of Ratramn's Theology | 40

Chapter 5
RATRAMN'S THEOLOGY OF TRANSFORMATION:
WHAT HAPPENS TO THE ELEMENTS? | 42
   The Act of Transformation—How Are
      the Elements Transformed? | 42
      The Crux—Change Only in the Spiritual Dimension | 42
      Analogs of Spiritual Change | 43
   The Result of Transformation—To What Are
      the Elements Transformed? | 45

Chapter 6
THE NATURE OF TRANSFORMATION: IS THE ACT
OF TRANSFORMATION A REPEATED SACRIFICE BY
CHRIST? | 51
   The Effect of the Transformation—How Do
      Communicants Respond? | 52
      The Objective Effect of the Transformation | 52
      The Subjective Response to the Transformation | 53

Chapter 7
THE PLACE OF RATRAMN IN THE DIACHRONIC DEVELOPMENT OF THE THEOLOGY OF THE EUCHARIST | 55
   Sources of Ratramn's Theology | 55
   Ratramn a Milestone in the Diachronic Development
      of Eucharistic Doctrine | 56

Chapter 8
CONCLUSION: CONTRASTS BETWEEN RADBERT
AND RATRAMN | 61
   Why Radbert's View Gained the Ascendancy
      until the Reformation | 62
   The Exegetical Continental Divide | 62

APPENDIX: A COMPARISON OF RADBERT'S
AND RATRAMN'S USE OF SUPPORTING SCRIPTURE | 65

 A. Radbert's Biblical Base—Proof Texts in the LCC edition
of *The Lord's Body and Blood* | 65
 B. Ratramn's Biblical Base—Proof Texts in the LCC edition
of *Christ's Body and Blood* | 67

BIBLIOGRAPHY | 71

RADBERTUS AND RATRAMNUS —THEIR CONTROVERSY REGARDING THE EUCHARIST

The books contained within the extensive catalogue written by my former student, friend, and fellow author-theologian Rev. Dr. George J. Gatgounis, Esq., share a common purpose—to provide practical answers and explanations to modern questions and issues through an examination of historical events and biblical evidence. This book's illumination of the Eucharistic controversy that divides the Protestant and Catholic perspectives makes it certainly deserving of its membership among such other great books as Dr. Gatgounis has written.

Within this work's pages, the reader will find a story expertly woven of the lives of two men—each of great integrity and strong spiritual connection with God and His Word, yet each having very different Eucharistic interpretations, out of which would quickly originate a profound and lasting tear in the very fabric of the visible Christianity. It is from great depths of examination and insight that Dr. Gatgounis brings us this work, and it is to his credit that the result is as readable as it is brilliant. Whether the reader be theologian, historian, clergy, seminarian—or whether he be not—all are invited to the feast; for indeed, it is the author's knack to bring forth remarkable produce from inexhaustible research that nourishes the soul of all who partake.

In contrast to the circumstances of Ratbertus and Ratramnus, my friend Dr. Gatgounis and I were never monastery-mates (although we frequently share a room assignment at the annual Evangelical Theological Society, Society of Biblical Literature, and American Academy of Religion). Over the course of many years, however, we developed a friendship that led to discovery of our own interpretive differences in regard to God's Word on matters non-essential to the faith. Such biblically defensible and valid interpretive differences between God's people are an inevitable reality in this world—interpretive differences within the matrix of visible Christianity are certain.

Through this work, Dr. Gatgounis provides a vehicle by which we may receive the author's gift of examination and deeper understanding of the origin and basis of this controversy, and as a result, a better understanding of one another. My prayer is that through this understanding, we will become a more informed body of Christ, appreciating, more fully, the true and full import of Jesus' words in the Eucharist, "This is my body."

H. Wayne House

INTRODUCTION

In the texture of the history of doctrine, Carolingians Radbertus and Ratramnus protrude as two juxtaposed exponents of divergent views of the elements of the Eucharist. Their polarity is a gauntlet to modern exegetes who must undertake the same interpretative challenges. A look back at this ninth-century bifurcation in the theology of the Eucharist orients the modern exegete to potential pitfalls. Appreciation of the historical/cultural context of the dueling Radbertus and Ratramnus requires some understanding of their intellectual setting.

WHO WERE THE CAROLINGIANS?

The Carolingians

The Carolingian dynasty was the medieval kingdom of the Franks which produced mayors of the palace (613–751), kings (751–987), and emperors (800–911) and is named for Emperor Charlemagne (768–814). Under the patronage of Charlemagne, a revival of learning in classical and patristic literature thrived. The Carolingian revival of learning included luminaries such as Alcuin of York (ca. 735–804) and Theodulf of Orleans (ca. 770–821), and in a second generation Rabanus Maurus (776–856) and his student Walafrid Strabo (809–849), who tutored Charles the Bald (840–877). Charles the Bald reigned as King of Aquitaine (843–877) and as Holy Roman Emperor (875–877).¹ The monastery at Corbie was the nest of Carolingian luminaries Radbertus (d. ca. 865; henceforward Radbert), Ratramnus (henceforward Ratramn), and Gottschalk. It was a vital intellectual center founded by Adalhard, the first cousin of Emperor Charlemagne, and later, the abbey of Corbie founded a smaller monastery, Corvey, in Saxony in 822.²

Among the Carolingian luminaries were Radbert and Ratramn. It was Ratramn of whom Charles the Bald asked about the nature of the elements of the Eucharist.³ Charles' questions may have generated from his reading of Radbert's *On the Body and the Blood of the Lord*. During the Carolingian Renaissance, the Eucharistic disagreement intensified because of Charles the Bald's inquiry of Ratramn as to whether the elements are Christ's actual body and blood *in veritate* or Christ's spiritual body and blood *in mysterio*. Charles also asked Ratramn whether the present body was the same body that "was born of Mary . . . died . . . and ascended into the heavens." In other words, Charles was inquiring whether the nature of the Eucharist was "nonsusbtantiation," "consubstantiation" or "transubstantiation". And, if it is transubstantiation, are the elements identical to Christ's historical body?⁴

Carolingian Academic Disciplines Significant to the Eucharistic Controversy

Significant to the Eucharistic controversy of Ratramn and Radbert is their use of grammar. The Carolingians, among them the earlier

---

1. John Fahey, *The Eucharistic Teaching of Ratramn of Corbie* (Mundelein, Ill.: Saint Mary of the Lake Seminary, 1951), 3.

2. Geoffrey W. Bromiley, *Historical Theology: An Introduction* (Grand Rapids: Wm. B. Eerdmans, 1978), 159; A. Wilmart, *Corbie, Dictionnaire d'Archeologie Chretienne et de Liturgie*, III, 2e partie, col. 2914.

3. C.M. Aherne, "Carolingian Renaissance" in *New Catholic Encyclopedia* (Washington, D.C.: Catholic University of America, 1967), 141–43.

4. Ratramnus, *De corp et sang. Dom.* 5 ed. J.N.B. van den Brink (Amsterdam: Noord-Hollandse Uitgervers Mig., 1954), 34; Julio L. Gonzalez, *A History of Christian Thought: From Augustine to the Eve of the Reformation* vol. 2 (Nashville: Abingdon, 1971), 117.

INTRODUCTION

Fredigisius, and as well the later Ratramn, perpetuated and enlarged the traditions of grammar as a school discipline—grammar continued to function as a leading method of theological scholarship.[5] The emphasis on the liberal arts in general, which included a vigorous emphasis on grammar, developed as a discipline among the Carolingians in part from Augustine's legacy. In *De Ordine*, for instance, Augustine argues for the utility of the liberal arts in unraveling theological problems.[6] In *De Ordine*, Augustine presupposes that the principle of order applies to all things. He then spells out a particular order for the study of the arts, which supplies data and methodology useful to the theologian.[7] Ratramn gave hearty support to Augustine's belief that liberal arts training cultivates the theological method.[8] The relation of grammar and theology among the Carolingians is significant because much of the polarity between the dueling monks derives from different interpretations of one specific figure of speech: "this is my body" (Matt. 26:27; Mark 14:23; Luke 22:17, 19).

Who Was Ratramn?

Ratramn was a monk at Corbie until 868. His first work was *On the Nativity* and was followed by *On Predestination*. His most significant work was *Against the Objections of the Greeks*, which is a polemic defending the filioque clause against the objections of Photius, Patriarch of Constantinople (858–867; 878–886).[9] Both Ratramn and John Scotus Erigena countered Radbert's views of

---

5. Marcia L. Colish, "Carolingian Debates over Nihil and Tenebrae: A Study in Theological Method," *Speculum* 59 (1984): 787. For an example of Ratramn's theological method, including the use of grammar in the Carolingian fashion, consider his refutation of the anonymous monk of Saint-Germer de Fly in Jean-Paul Bouhot, *Ratramne de Corbie: Histoire letteraire et controverses doctrinales* (Paris, 1976), 57–60 and D. C. Lambot, *Liber de anima ad Odonem Bellovacensem, Analecta mediaevalia Namurcensia* 2 (Namur, 1951): 8–11.

6. Colish, "Carolingian Debates over Nihil and Tenebrae," 758.

7. Ibid., 757.

8. Ibid., 758.

9. Bromiley, *Historical Theology: An Introduction*, 162.

the nature of the Eucharistic elements, but Erigena's work was burned by papal order at Vercelli in 1059.[10]

Who Was Radbert?

Unfortunately, history has many gaps in the life of Radbert. Radbert, fond of calling himself "of all monks the scum,"[11] forbad his understudies to compose his biography.[12] Radbert came to Corbie under its first abbot, Adalhard, and was himself later elected its fourth abbot in 844. Resigning in 853, Radbert devoted himself to study until his decease in 865. His works include five books of commentaries on Lamentations and fourteen books of commentaries on Matthew, an exposition of Psalm 44, a treatise defending the special birth of Jesus, short treatments of three theological virtues, and biographies of the first two abbots, Adalhard and his brother Wala.[13]

Specifically, the major contributions of Radbert include *Expositio in evangelium Matthaei*,[14] addressed to the monk Guntland, *Expositio in Psalmum* 45 [=44 (R.S.V.)],[15] which is addressed to the nuns of St. Mary of Soissons who had educated Radbert in his youth, and *In threnos sive lamentationes Ieremiae v*,[16] (addressed to Odilmannus Severus). Radbert's shorter works include *Opusculum de partu Virginis (On the Virgin Birth)*,[17] addressed to a nun of Soissons, *De fide, spe et charitate libri iii (Faith, Hope, and Charity)*,[18]

---

10. Nicholas Ridley, *A Brief Declaration of the Lord's Supper* ed. H.C.G. Moule (reprint ed., New York: Thomas Whittaker, 1895), 204 (editor's comment, Appendix 1).

11. Bromiley, *Historical Theology: An Introduction*, 90.

12. Bromiley, *Historical Theology: An Introduction*, 91.

13. Bromiley, *Historical Theology: An Introduction*, 159.

14. *Patrologia Latina* (hereafter MPL), ed. J.P. Migne, 217 vols., indexes 4 vols. (Paris 1878-90), 31.994.

15. MPL 120.993-1060.

16. MPL 120.1059-1256.

17. MPL 120.1365-1386.

18. MPL 120.1387-1490.

INTRODUCTION

(addressed to Warin, introduced by an acrostic poem "*Radbert Levita*"), and *De passione SS Rufini et Valerii* (*The Passion of Saints Rufinus and Valerius*).[19] Radbert's biographical works include *Vita Sancti Adalhardi Corbeiensis abbatis* (*Life of Saint Adalhard*)[20] and *Epitaphium Arsenii seu vita venerabilis Walae abbatis Corbeiensis in Gallia* (*Symposium in memory of Adalhard's brother Wala*).[21] Radbert wrote his defense of transubstantiation in *The Lord's Body and Blood* in 831 and sent a final edited version to Charles the Bald as a Christmas gift in 844.[22]

19. MPL 120.1489–1508.
20. MPL 120.1507–1508.
21. MPL 120.1557–1650.
22. Bromiley, *Historical Theology: An Introduction*, 159. Radbert's contribution to the development of Marian theology, particularly the alleged assumption of Mary, includes a letter, ostensibly authored by Jerome to his friends Paul and Eustochium, but has correctly been ascribed to Radbert. Regarding the authenticity of the letter, Knowles remarks that "no one familiar with Jerome's style or the liturgy could be deceived for a moment. Erasmus, "first to smell a rat, extrapolated that the letter was probably translated from seventh-century Greek. The letter did little to further Marian theology, however." The work Der pseudo-Hieronymus-Brief IX, '*Cogitis me*': *Ein erster Marianischer Traktat des Mittelalters von Paschasius Radbert*, ed. Albert Ripberger (Frieburg, Schweiz: Universitatsverlag, 1962), *Journal of Theological Studies*, n.s., 15 (April 1964):183–84, argues conclusively that the letter was written by Radbert. "Cogitis me" was written by Radbert (in the person of Jerome) to Abbess Theodrada of Soissons and her daughter Imma (as Paulea and Eustochium), and was intended to stimulate devotion to the Blessed Virgin while maintaining a reserved attitude towards the opinion held in some circles that the body of Mary as well as her soul was taken up at her Assumption. The letter, essentially a sermon, leans on a variety of authorities, including Cassian, Ambrose, and Leo the Great, but is "non-committal if not unfriendly towards the assertion of bodily assumption, nevertheless puts forward most of the arguments ex convenientia subsequently used to commend the opinion which ultimately won its way." David Knowles, review of *Der pseudo-Hieronymus-Brief IX, 'Cogitis me': Ein erster Marianischer Traktat des Mittelalters von Paschasius Radbert*. Compare Yarnold's skepticism as to who wrote de benedictionibus Patriarcharum which bears the name Rodbertus as author. Although Yarnold does not doubt Rodbertus refers to Radbertus, he leaves authenticity in doubt. E.J. Yarnold, review of *Pascasii Radberti: De Benedictionibus Patriarcharum Jacob et Moysi*, ed. Bedae Paulus. (Turnhout: Brepois, 1993), *Journal of Theological Studies*, n.s., 45 (April 1994):368–69.

THE EUCHARISTIC CONTROVERSY AMONG OTHER CAROLINGIANS

Several literary works attest to a concern for a more uniform understanding of the nature of the consecrated elements among Carolinian theologians.[23] Rabanus Maurus, Archbishop of Mainz and Abbot of Fulda, warned Heribald of Auxerre (ca. 855) against those "who, incorrectly judging, recently have said that the sacrament of the body and blood of the Lord is the same body and blood of the Lord which was born of the virgin Mary, and which suffered on the cross, and which is risen from the grave."[24] On the other hand, John Scotus Erigena, titular head of the palace school in Laon, cautioned "about those who wish to assert the visible Eucharist to signify nothing else but itself."[25] But Gottschalk, the nomadic monk eventually exiled from Hautvillers because of his predestinarian views, focused his work as a rebuttal to Radbert in *De corpore et sanguine domini*. In sum, to Gottschalk, the realism of Radbert bordered on cannibalism, causing Christ to suffer repeatedly.[26]

Although the work of Rabanus Maurus on this work has been lost, Rabanus sided with Gottschalk and Ratramn against

---

23. Gary Macy, *The Theologies of the Eucharist in the Early Scholastic Period: A Study of the Salvific Function of the Sacrament according to the Theologians c. 1080–c. 1220* (Oxford: Clarendon Press, 1984), 22.

24. Macy, *The Theologies of the Eucharist in the Early Scholastic Period: A Study of the Salvific Function of the Sacrament according to the Theologians c. 1080–c. 1220*, 23; Epistola 56 (Monumenta Germaniae historica, Epistolae, 5, 513).

25. Macy, *The Theologies of the Eucharist in the Early Scholastic Period: A Study of the Salvific Function of the Sacrament according to the Theologians c. 1080–c. 1220*, 23; *Expositiones in ierarchiam coelestem*, cap. 1 (ed. J. Barbet, Corpus christianorum, continuatio medievalis, 31 (Turnhout, 1975): 17.

26. Macy, *The Theologies of the Eucharist in the Early Scholastic Period: A Study of the Salvific Function of the Sacrament according to the Theologians c. 1080–c. 1220*, 23; *De corpore et sanguine domini* (ed. C. Lambot, OEuvres theologique et grammaticales de Godescalc d'Orbais Spicilegium sacrum lovaniense, 20 (Louvain, 1945): 324–26.

Radbert.[27] John Scotus Erigena, although marginal to the debate, also sided with Ratramn.[28] Rabanus Maurus rejected Radbert's claim that the elements transubstantiate into the actual body, which was virgin born, suffered, and rose. Rabanus argued that the elements became the actual body and blood of Christ, but "in some different state and mode of presence from His state in His life on earth and His mode of presence in the glory of His heavenly life."[29]

To be sure, the treatises of Radbert and Ratramn on the Eucharist are juxtaposed, but this juxtaposition of the works does not necessarily imply they were opposing centerpieces of theological camps. Radbert's work was perhaps available to Ratramn for some fourteen years prior his writing his work, and Ratramn does not appear to answer Radbert's points *ad seriatim*, but rather addresses specific questions posed to him by Charles the Bald. Further, no councils were called, nor any condemnations ensued. Actually, the distinctive theologies of Radbert and Ratramn apparently co-existed harmoniously at the monastery of Corbie.[30]

SCOPE AND STATEMENT OF THESIS

Delimitations

This study concerns the conflicting viewpoints of Radbert and Ratramn as to the exact nature of the consecrated elements in the Eucharist. Accordingly, there are some limitations that confine the scope of this study. The first of these issues is whether water should be mixed with wine and whether a fragment of bread should be

27. Gonzalez, *A History of Christian Thought: From Augustine to the Eve of the Reformation*, 119.

28. Gonzalez, *A History of Christian Thought: From Augustine to the Eve of the Reformation*, 119; John Scotus Erigena, Exp. auper Ierarch. cael. 1.

29. Darwell Stone, *A History of the Doctrine of the Holy Eucharist* (New York: Longmans, Green, and Co., 1909), II:223.

30. Macy, *The Theologies of the Eucharist in the Early Scholastic Period: A Study of the Salvific Function of the Sacrament according to the Theologians c. 1080–c. 1220*, 21–22.

dipped in wine are outside the parameters of this study. Second, this study is not concerned whether spiritual benefit changes according to the mass (quantity) of the element. Third, whether the worthiness of the administrator of the sacrament may obviate or disaffect the rite is outside the consideration of this study. Fourth, whether a fast before the rite or culmination of a meal (love feast, *cf.* Jude 12)[31] by the rite is exegetically warranted is outside this purview.

Rather, this study circumscribes Ratramn's and Radbert's particular works on the Eucharist. Their other works are cited only to inform understanding of their Eucharistic treatises. This study delves into the theology of transformation of the elements of the Eucharist according to the conflicting perspectives of Radbert and Ratramn. The burden of this study is to be informative of the controversy, not polemic for either side.

Statement of Thesis

While both Radbert and Ratramn believe in a real transformation of the consecrated Eucharistic elements, they disagree on the resultant physical composition of the elements. Ratramn correctly argues that the transformation results in a spiritually real presence of Christ's body and blood. However, Radbert argues incorrectly that the transformation results in elements that are physically comprised of Christ's historical and actual body and blood.

---

31. Albert Schweitzer, *The Lord's Supper in Relationship to the Life of Jesus and the History of the Early Church* (Macon, Ga.: Mercer University, 1982), 95. To the ancient church, the Didache records the Lord's Supper as a "joyful meal."

Chapter 1

THE INTERRELATION OF RADBERT AND RATRAMN ON THE NATURE OF THE EUCHARISTIC ELEMENTS

WHO IS RESPONDING TO WHOM?

The most thorough treatment of Ratramn's Eucharistic views is John F. Fahey's *The Eucharistic Teaching of Ratramn of Corbie*. In it Fahey argues that Ratramn and Radbert must be understood in relation to each other:

> It is no more misleading to quote a sentence out of context than it is to study a controversial book apart from its historical setting . . . like so many pieces of a jig-saw puzzle, the individual treatises seem misshapen and patternless until fitted together.[1]

To Fahey, a point/counterpoint relation between the two theologians is "historical fact."[2]

Moreover, Fahey believes beyond any doubt that Ratramn wrote his treatise around 850 to offer an alternative theological model to ever-growing transubstantiationism articulated in

---

1. Fahey, *The Eucharistic Teaching of Ratramn of Corbie*, 2.
2. Fahey, *The Eucharistic Teaching of Ratramn of Corbie*, 165.

Radbert's first edition written in 831 (which was revised to its final form in 844).³ But Fahey believes Radbert wrote with Ratramn's teachings in mind, at least from an oral tradition. If Fahey's historical reconstruction is correct, Radbert fixed Ratramn as his adversary, furthering the personal and political forces that had already driven them into different positions.⁴ Personally, Radbert was an abbot and teacher who focused primarily on instruction of the plain folk, and his treatise was designed to be read by the unlettered faithful—while Ratramn was an erudite scholarly monk who purposed to suffuse himself with Augustine.⁵ To Fahey, the theological disagreement became another dimension of distance between them.⁶

Calogero Gliozzo disagrees with Fahey, however. He argues that Radbert indeed wrote first but with an another adversary in mind: "Paschase [Radbert], it is true, speaks of adversaries who oppose his doctrine; it seems, however, that he is referring to discourses made against him rather than to written words."⁷ Gliozzo elaborates:

> We may conclude that the adversaries of Paschase [Radbert] are not found together with him, because he had heard of their objections, that they were men more talkative than learned, and that Paschase knew of no work written in his time, which contained an error concerning the Eucharist.⁸

---

3. Fahey, *The Eucharistic Teaching of Ratramn of Corbie*, 11.
4. cf. Fahey, *The Eucharistic Teaching of Ratramn of Corbie*, 11.
5. cf. Fahey, *The Eucharistic Teaching of Ratramn of Corbie*, 163–64.
6. Fahey, *The Eucharistic Teaching of Ratramn of Corbie*, 11.
7. Calogero Gliozzo quoted in Fahey, *The Eucharistic Teaching of Ratramn of Corbie*, 4. After having proved by means of the words of consecration the identity of the "sacramental Body of Christ and His historical Body," Radbert writes: "haec prolixius dixerim quia audivi quosdam me reprehendere, quasi ego in eo libro, quem de Sacramentis Christi edideram, aliquid, his dictis plus tribuere voluerim, aut aliud quam ipsa Verits repromittit." PL t. 120, (ca. 1357).
8. Gliozzo quoted in Fahey, *The Eucharistic Teaching of Ratramn of Corbie*, 5.

THE INTERRELATION OF RADBERT AND RATRAMN

Because Ratramn was a scholar resident at Corbie, Gliozzo concludes that Radbert, who wrote first, had some other adversary(s) in mind. Accordingly, Charles, perhaps curious about the fantastic narratives in Radbert's treatise, asked Ratramn for clarification because Ratramn was an Augustinian scholar.[9]

Fahey rebuts Gliozzio, however, because Radbert identified his adversary on the issue of the nature of Mary's childbirth as "one of his brethren."[10] Fahey thinks the only "one of his brethren" who ever publicly opposed Radbert was Ratramn. Accordingly, Fahey concludes Radbert wrote first, responding to Ratramn's oral teaching.[11]

COMMON GROUND AND POINT OF DIVERGENCE

Regardless of who is responding to whom, the interrelation between Ratramn's and Radbert's works on the Eucharist is a divergence not without common ground. This common ground includes both Ratramn and Radbert calling for faith, stressing divine power, agreeing that Christ's body is present to give life, and affirming the role of the Word and Holy Spirit.[12] The specific point of disagreement between the two scholars is the relation of the Eucharist to Christ's historical body.[13] Ratramn argued against the doctrine advanced by various unknown German teachers that Christ was naturally born, but "broke forth miraculously." Prudent that the doctrine of miraculous birth would lead to docetism, Ratramn defended a natural birth (per vulvam) of Jesus which

---

9. Gonzalez, *A History of Christian Thought: From Augustine to the Eve of the Reformation*, 119.

10. Fahey, *The Eucharistic Teaching of Ratramn of Corbie*, 7.

11. Fahey, *The Eucharistic Teaching of Ratramn of Corbie*, 163. However, Radbert definitely later offered his rebuttal to Ratramn's work in his Letter to Frudergard.

12. cf. Ratramn, "Ratramnus of Corbie: Christ's Body and Blood," *Library of Christian Classics* (hereafter LCC), vol. 9, paragraphs 17 and 22 (hereafter sections signified by Roman numerals; paragraphs signified by "()").

13. Fahey, *The Eucharistic Teaching of Ratramn of Corbie*, 165.

neither contaminated Him nor obviated Mary's virginity, and argued for the perpetual virginity of Mary, "before the birth, in the birth, and after the birth."[14] In opposition to this, Radbert argued against this natural birth view of Ratramn, holding that since postfall natural childbirth is under the curse, Jesus' birth was not on par with other births.[15] The divergence between them involves the physical composition of the elements of the Eucharist.

---

14. Gonzalez, *A History of Christian Thought: From Augustine to the Eve of the Reformation*, 115.

15. Radbertus, *De partu Virg.* 1 (PL, 120:1368–69). For a collection of the most significant texts, see S. Bonano, "The Divine Maternity and the Eucharistic Body and the Doctrine of Paschasius Radbertus," *EphemMar*, 1 (1951):379–94. Hincmar of Reims later agreed that Jesus had not been born in the same manner as other children. Hincmar, De div. Lot. et Tet. 12. Gonzalez, *A History of Christian Thought: From Augustine to the Eve of the Reformation*, 117.

Chapter 2

RADBERT'S VIEW OF THE ELEMENTS IN THE EUCHARIST

THE NATURE OF THE EUCHARIST

What Is a Sacrament in General?

Radbert defines a sacrament[1] as "any divine celebration as a pledge of salvation, when what is visibly done accomplishes inwardly something far different . . ."[2] Attendant to the act of the sacrament is an "oath," in which each communicant "takes sides" in making an agreement with God.[3] Radbert calls the Eucharist a "mysterion,"[4] appealing to the Greek semantic sense by using a term that connotes something of hidden and secret character.[5] Radbert calls the sacraments "mysteries" because of the secrecy of the acts of the Spirit—the Spirit "latently accomplishes" the acts "under the cover things visible."[6] To Radbert, "'truth' is anything

1. LCC, 98 (III.1).
2. LCC, 98 (III.1).
3. LCC, 98 (III.2).
4. LCC, 99 (III.2).
5. LCC, 99 (III.2).
6. LCC, 98 (III.1).

rightly understood or believed inwardly concerning this mystery."[7] Thus, the work of the Spirit in the Eucharist is latent in two dimensions: the elements are transformed under their visible appearance; and the elements impart inward spiritual nourishment to the communicant.

According to Radbert, ongoing regeneration results through spiritually ingesting the newly created flesh and blood of Christ.[8] Through the Eucharist believers are "invigorated by tasting him ... prepared for things immortal and eternal ... [and] made one in Christ."[9] As a worthy communicant is physically nourished so are they also spiritually nourished through implantation of eternal life.

Radbert believes that the incarnation is the great sacrament, "because in the visible man the divine majesty inwardly ... worked invisibly those things which came into being secretly by his power." In the "great sacrament" we are pardoned, but in baptism "a door for entering into adoption is opened for believers."[10] Although he calls the incarnation the great sacrament, Radbert recognizes but two sacraments per se. His contemporary Rabanus Maurus added extreme unction. Not until the Scholastics, under Peter Lombard's influence (d. 1164), did seven sacraments find consensus.[11] As the Holy Spirit illumines believers through the Word, similarly He illumines believers through the sacraments.[12]

---

7. LCC, 102 (IV.2).
8. LCC (III.4).
9. LCC (III.4).
10. LCC (III.2).
11. LCC, 99. n. 30.
12. LCC (III.4).

RADBERT'S THEOLOGY OF TRANSFORMATION— WHAT HAPPENS TO THE ELEMENTS?

The Means of Transformation

Radbert resolves any difficulties attendant to the transformation through reference to divine omnipotence[13] and human faith. Radbert explains how the elements, which appear identical after the words of predication,[14] become the actual body and blood of Christ: "the body and blood of Christ is created by the power of the Spirit in his word . . ."[15] The elements may be transformed into the actual body and blood of Christ because with "God nothing is impossible."[16] Miraculous power makes the transformation possible.[17]

Accordingly, Radbert urges faith over reason to comprehend the miracle of transformation. He expresses that the means of transformation is beyond our reason:

13. Macy, *The Theologies of the Eucharist in the Early Scholastic Period: A Study of the Salvific Function of the Sacrament according to the Theologians c. 1080–c. 1220*, 28.

14. Zwingli and Schwenkfeld argue that the words of predication, "this is my body," are parabolic, in the same vein as "the field is the word" (Mt. 13:38), "the seed is the Word of God" (Lk. 8:11), "the bones are the whole house of Israel" (Ez. 37:11), "the two olive branches" (Zech. 4:11), and "the seven candlesticks are the seven churches" (Rev. 1:20). Martin Chemnitz, *The Lord's Supper*, trans. J.A.O. Preus, reprint ed., *De coena Domoni, 1590* (St. Louis: Concordia Publishing House, 1979), 49. Similarly appropriate would be parabolic words of predication in Numbers 5:17–19, "these are the bitter words that cause the curse," Matthew 3:13, and "this is the Holy Spirit," and 2 Kings 2:11–12, "these are the angels of God." Gustaf Aulen argues that veneration of the bread, artolatreia, as a result of the words of predication is unwarranted because biblical examples of actual transformation are different. For example, in Exodus 4 and 7, the rod transforms into a serpent and in John 2 the water transforms into wine. In contradistinction, Christ treats the allegedly transformed elements as if they are still what they appear to be (Lk. 22:17; 1 Cor. 11:25). Gustaf Aulen, *Eucharist and Sacrifice*, trans. Eric H. Wahlstrom (Phil.: Muhlenberg Press, 1958), 51.

15. LCC, 102 (IV.1).

16. LCC (I.4).

17. cf. Bromiley, *Historical Theology: An Introduction*, 160.

> If you ask the method, who can explain or express it in words? Be assured, please, that the method resides in Christ's virtue, the knowledge of faith, the cause in power, but the effect in will, because the power of divinity effectively works beyond the power of our reason.[18]

He charges his readers not to be astounded at the miraculous transformation:

> Do not be surprised, O man, and do not ask about the order of nature here; but if you truly believe that flesh was without seed created from the Virgin Mary in her womb by the power of the Holy Spirit, so that the Word might be made flesh, truly believe also that what is constructed in the Christ's word through the Holy Spirit is his body from the Virgin.[19]

Radbert thereby urges perception by faith, not sight, citing 1 Corinthians 10:3.[20]

THE NATURE OF THE CONSECRATED ELEMENTS

The Consecrated Elements Actually Transubstantiated

To Radbert, the consecrated elements are both in truth and in a figure the body and blood of Christ.[21] After consecration, the elements are "nothing but" the flesh and blood of Christ.[22] Hincmar of Rheims (806–882) agreed with Radbert, on the "effect of consecration in making the elements the body and blood of Christ by virtue of the creative power of God there exercised as in the conception by the Virgin and the miracles of the Old Testament . . . so that the whole Christ is entirely present in each fragment

---

18. LCC, 103 (IV.3).
19. LCC, 103 (IV.3).
20. LCC, 103 (IV.3).
21. LCC, 102 (IV.2).
22. Radbertus, quoted in Gonzalez, A *History of Christian Thought: From Augustine to the Eve of the Reformation*, 118.

of the Sacrament."[23] Radbert sees the elements actually transmute: "in truth the body and blood are created by the consecration of the mystery,"[24] and argues that the elements, under their visible appearance, are divine flesh "secretly hallowed through power, so that they are inwardly in truth what they are outwardly believed to be by the power of faith."[25] After the consecration the elements are "nothing but Christ's flesh and blood[26] . . . to put it into miraculous terms, nothing different, of course, from what was born of Mary, suffered on the cross, and rose again from the tomb."[27] The elements are "spiritual things," created flesh and blood of Christ by invisible power.[28] Radbert asks, "What is it that men eat?"[29] and then answers "the bread is the Body of the Lord in respect of its being, out and out, the identical body of the Incarnation."[30] As the divinity and body of Christ are consubstantial, according to Radbert, so the elements and the body of Christ are related.[31] Because the elements are Christ's literal body and blood, they have "eternal

---

23. Stone, *A History of the Doctrine of the Holy Eucharist*, II:233. Haymo (778–853), Abbot of Hersfeld, also adopted Radbert's position, that the "nature of bread and wine, is substantially converted into another susbtance, that is, into flesh and blood. . . . According to a letter of Haymo, "the invisible Priest changes His visible creatures into the substance of His flesh and blood by his unseen power." Stone, *Doctrine of the Holy Eucharist*, II:234.

24. LCC, 101 (IV.1).

25. LCC, 99 (III.1).

26. LCC, 94 (I.2). Compare this to Ambrose: "Perhaps you will say, 'My bread is common (bread).' But that bread is bread before the words of the sacrament; when consecration has been applied, from (being) bread it becomes the flesh of Christ." Ambrose, as quoted by R.C.D. Jasper and G.J. Cuming, *Prayers of the Eucharist: Early and Reformed* (New York: Oxford University Press, 1980), 112.

27. LCC, 94 (I.2).

28. LCC, 101 (III. 4).

29. LCC, 106 (2), line 1.

30. Ridley, *A Brief Declaration of the Lord's Supper*, 202.

31. LCC, 102 (III.2).

life abiding in them,"[32] although they are the same as their earlier corporeal appearance and taste.[33]

In his later commentary on Matthew, Radbert would rebut Ratramn, declaring that Ratramn posits the sacrament has "power of the flesh and not the flesh; the power of the blood, and not the blood; the figure and not the truth; the shadow and not the body."[34] Radbert thinks that the Lord himself refuted Ratramn's faulty view, saying "this is my body which is given for you."[35]

J. Pohle expresses the opinion that Radbert is in error and accuses him of "a grossly carnal Capharnaite-like apprehension."[36] Is the body of Christ physically, bodily, and outwardly ingested by the communicant through mastication, digestion, and absorption? Augustine and Cyril said no, arguing against others at Capernaum who believed the body of Christ is decimated and distributed like meat of cattle at a meat market.[37] Augustine declaimed against "Scythian cannabalism" (anqrwpofagia).[38] Paschasius in a lengthy sermon rejects the doctrine of Capharnaite flesh eating (sarkofagia).[39] Augustine, Cyril, and later Ratramn would rebut

32. LCC, 95 (I.5).

33. LCC, 95 (I.5).

34. In Matt. Evang. 9.26 (PL 120:890); Gonzalez, *A History of Christian Thought: From Augustine to the Eve of the Reformation*, 119.

35. Matt. Evang. 9.26 (PL 120:890); Gonzalez, *A History of Christian Thought: From Augustine to the Eve of the Reformation*, 119.

36. J. Pohle, CE 11.518.

37. Probably Homily 9, *De poenitentia, Patriologia Graeca*, ed. J. P. Migne, 161 vols. (Paris, 1857–1866) [MPG]49:343–50, particularly 345. Origin in Matthew 15 rejects a supernaturalist view of the elements, explaining that "the sanctified bread according to its material aspects goes out with the waste and is ejected by the digestive process. But Chrysostom says in *De encoeniis*, "does the rest of the food go out through the digestive process? God forbid!" Aulen, *Eucharist and Sacrifice*, 59. Gregory of Nyssa, for instance, demonstrated that without a hint of cannabilism the Christian spiritually feeds upon Christ in the Eucharist. Bromiley, *Historical Theology: An Introduction*, 160.

38. Aulen, *Eucharist and Sacrifice*, 59; cf. *Contra adversarium legis et prophetarum*, MPL 42.658.

39. Aulen, *Eucharist and Sacrifice*, 59; *De corpore et sanguine Domini*, MPL 120.1267–1350.

that Radbert "literalizes" the figure of speech "this is my body"[40] and misapplies 1 Corinthians 10:3 by claiming that sight and reason must contradict faith.

The Reason the Transubstantiated Elements Appear the Same

The reason why the transmogrified elements appear the same, according to Radbert, is that "faith may be proved in spirit."[41] If the communicant desires the blessing of the Eucharist, then the communicant must believe the elements are different, even though they appear to be empirically the same. Faith over the senses, to Radbert, is the requisite epistemology.[42] Although Radbert refers to the bread element in the "Mass"[43] as a "wafer,"[44] Radbert believes a special concession applies to those who fervently love the Lord, enabling them to see the "true color" of flesh and blood.[45]

Geoffrey Bromiley sees the appearance/substance dichotomy as "a tantalizing obscurity":[46]

> Is he claiming that Christ's incarnate body replaces the elements, so that the senses deceive us when they see only the elements? Or does he mean that, as in the incarnation, faith sees something senses do not see, the deity as well as the humanity, the body and blood as well as the bread and wine.[47]

---

40. Peter Martyr Vermigli held that Christ might "well have said: This signifieth or betokeneth my body, or this respecteth my body, or this is a figure of my body, or this is a sign and token of my body" Peter Martyr Vermigli, *The Discourse of Peter Martyr upon the Sacrament of the Lord's Supper* (1550, photostat by University Microfilms, Ann Arbor, Michigan), fol. iiii, para. iv.

41. LCC, 95 (I.5).

42. cf. Bromiley, *Historical Theology: An Introduction*, 160.

43. LCC, 107 (VI.3).

44. LCC, 106 (VI.2).

45. Radbertus, *De corp. et sang. Dom.* 14; Gonzalez, *A History of Christian Thought: From Augustine to the Eve of the Reformation*, 118.

46. Bromiley, *Historical Theology: An Introduction*, 161.

47. Bromiley, *Historical Theology: An Introduction*, 161–62.

Radbert does not explain why it is that only by faith can an actual transformation into the body and blood of Christ be seen.[48] The elements are subject to intelligible and sensual perception. But, is there a contradiction between faith and understanding? Radbert counters this outlook by saying that to view the consecrated elements according to sensual perception is ignorance. Radbert declaims Christ "frees us from all ignorance."[49]

The Truth/Figure Distinction in the Elements

Radbert argues that the truth/appearance distinction regarding the elements does not render the figure mendacious.[50] Radbert explains that a figure need not be a mere shadow or a falsity. Under Bromiley's analysis, to Radbert, his fear "of Eucharistic docetism or dualism rules out all concept of a spiritual feeding which is not also bodily."[51]

ANALOGS TO THE ELEMENTS

The Comparison of New Testament Truth and Old Testament Figure

Radbert thinks that as the Spirit created from the virgin a true body for Christ, so the same Spirit re-creates the body and blood of Christ in the Eucharist.[52] This re-creation Radbert calls the "mystical consecration."[53] Regarding this transformation, "the method resides in Christ's virtue, the knowledge in faith, the cause in power, the effect in will."[54] Radbert contrasts Old Testament

---

48. Bromiley, *Historical Theology: An Introduction*, 162.
49. Bromiley, *Historical Theology: An Introduction*, 160.
50. cf. LCC, 102 (IV.2).
51. Bromiley, *Historical Theology: An Introduction*, 160.
52. LCC (IV.1).
53. LCC (IV.1).
54. LCC (IV.3).

(OT) figures from the New Testament (NT) figures—the old were mere shadows but the new are "truth"—*in veritate*. "Created by the power of the Spirit," the NT figure is real.[55] The analog for the consecrated elements, to Radbert, is the body of Christ, which is "holy truth and no shadow."[56] Although pedagogical, the figure is *in veritate*.

The body and blood foreshadowed in OT symbols are now mysteries of truth fulfilled.[57] Radbert compares the elements to the tree of life, "from which the state of man might have continued forever."[58] Because of the resurrection[59] the earlier figures of manna and the Paschal lamb are passed away, being superseded by the "true" figures, the body and blood of Christ.

Radbert calls manna a type of the food of Christ's body with the water being an analog of the water and blood from Christ's riven side.[60] "The bread of angels" analogy implies that "man lives on what angels live on because everything is spiritual and divine in what man receives."[61] This compares with Cyprian who said in *De coena Domini*: "We eat the bread of angels in the Sacrament here on earth, and we will eat the same without the Sacrament in heaven, but not by means of a bodily ministry, repeatedly returning to it, but the completed sacrificial work of Christ will remain permanent and be established, with His sufficiency filling and refreshing us because of the fact that He offered Himself openly and without any covering, in the sight of all performing the highest sacrifice."[62] Radbert calls the partaking of this food a feeding on "angelic grace."[63]

---

55. LCC (IV.1).
56. LCC (IV.2).
57. LCC, 104 (V.1).
58. LCC, 95 (I.6).
59. LCC (V.1).
60. LCC, 104 (V.1).
61. LCC, 104 (V.1).
62. Aulen, *Eucharist and Sacrifice*, 51.
63. LCC, 100 (III.4).

The Analogy of Baptism

Radbert relates the Eucharist to baptism analogously. In baptism, according to Radbert, "a door for entering into adoption is opened for believers" which is a rebirth, freeing one from evil.[64] From baptism onward, the Holy Spirit is poured out upon the one being reborn. The result of the Spirit's outpouring is the quickening of the entire body into a single spirit.[65] Radbert, in a single sentence, affirms baptismal regeneration and the continuous nature of Eucharistic regeneration: "in the baptism through the water we are from him all regenerated, and afterward we daily feed upon Christ's body and drink his blood by his power."[66]

The Analogy of the Written Word of God

Radbert analogizes the relation of the elements with Christ's actual body with the relation of the letters of the words of Scripture with the words' referent.[67] As a child learns to read, the child advances from understanding the amalgam of letters to the apprehension of the words' referents. Through the words of Scripture the child later apprehends God. Similarly, the communicant sees the elements, then "there is a progression from the humanity of Christ to the divinity of the Father."[68] Radbert equates the sacraments with the Holy Scriptures as equivalent agents of the Holy Spirit, who "inwardly works the mysteries of our salvation unto immortality."[69]

---

64. LCC, 99 (III.2).
65. LCC, 99 (III.2).
66. LCC, 101 (III.4).
67. LCC, 102 (III.2).
68. LCC, 102 (IV.2).
69. LCC, 95 (I.4).

The Analogy of the Incarnation

Radbert sees the incarnation as a "great sacrament," because the divine majesty became visible man secretly by his divine power.[70] In both sacraments, the Supper and the incarnation, according to Radbert, we are "redeemed unto pardon," being instructed and empowered to "pass from the condition" of death unto life.

The Analogy of Sacrifice

Radbert thinks that "mystical consecration" repeats that actual sacrifice of Christ—that is, Christ suffers and dies in every celebration.[71] To Radbert, the Eucharist is a sacrifice, because:

> in it the Church on earth offers prayer through the instrumentality of the ministering priest. When at the consecration the bread and wine are made to be the body and blood of Christ by the power of the Lord and of the Holy Ghost, they are uplifted into the heavenly sphere, presented on the heavenly altar of the body of Christ, offered by Christ as His own sacrifice, and given back by Him to the communicants on earth as supernatural food.[72]

On the other hand, Gottschalk opposed Radbert's theory of repetitious sacrifice,[73] arguing rather for a "mysterious presence,"[74]

70. LCC, 99 (III.2).

71. Radbertus, *De corp. et sang. Dom.* 9.1; Gonzalez, *A History of Christian Thought: From Augustine to the Eve of the Reformation*, 118; Richard Stanley Haugh, *The Byzantine-Carolingian Triadological Controversy with a View toward its Appeal to Tradition and the Fathers* (unpublished doctoral dissertation, Fordham University, 1973).

72. Stone, *A History of the Doctrine of the Holy Eucharist*, II: 220.

73. Justin regarded the Eucharist as a sacrifice of thanksgiving and praise. Aulen, *Eucharist and Sacrifice*, 180. Irenaeus saw the bread and wine as the offered first fruits of creation, whereas Cyprian referred to the eucharist as a sacrifice, but may call it a sacrifice in that what is inherent in the supper is inherent in Christ himself, who was the sacrifice. Aulen, *Eucharist and Sacrifice*, 180.

74. Peter Martyr explained that "if anyone by the term 'presence'

whose core is a "power of the Word" active in the believer.[75] Gottschalk's view compares to Irenaeus' view of the role of the word in the sacrament in *Adversus haereses*, which argues: "Christ has testified that the cup which is a created thing is His blood, and He has confirmed that the bread which is a created thing is His body, from which our bodies draw strength." Irenaues further elaborates: "Therefore when the mixed chalice and the bread receive the Word of God, there is a Eucharist of the blood and body of Christ, from which the substance of our flesh draws strength and whereby it exists."[76]

---

understands the grasping by faith whereby we ourselves ascend into heaven and lay hold on Christ in His majesty with our mind and our spirit, then I am in agreement with him." Aulen, *Eucharist and Sacrifice*, 42.

75. Gonzalez, *A History of Christian Thought: From Augustine to the Eve of the Reformation*, 119.

76. Irenaeus, *Adversus haereses*, Bk. 5, ch. 2. "How can they deny that the flesh is capable of receiving this gift of God, which is life eternal, since it is nourished by the blood and body of Christ and made His member, as the apostle says 'Since we are members of His body, of His flesh and of His bone' [Eph. 5:30]? It is not of some spiritual or invisible man that he says these things, for 'a spirit does not have flesh and bones' [Lk. 24:39], but he is speaking of that quality which is characteristic of a human being, who is made up of flesh and nerves and is nourished by the cup which is His blood and bread which is His body."

Chapter 3

THE RESULT OF WORTHY PARTAKING OF THE ELEMENTS

Radbert articulates a twofold rule of participation: first, the communicant must "discern" the Lord's body, that is, "what the sacrament is, or how great it is, what sort of power it has . . ." Then he must test himself as to "whether he is in Christ's body, or if Christ remains in him."[1]

DESCRIPTION OF THE REQUISITE WORTHINESS—TO BE IN CHRIST

Partaking of the sacrament worthily is to remain in Christ and Christ to remain in him.[2] Radbert identifies the individual who actually is in Christ:

> he therefore remains in Christ who, reborn from water and Spirit, is held guilty of no mortal offense,[3] and in him [remains] Christ who opened to him the door of faith through consecration by the Holy Spirit, so that he

---

1. LCC, 106 (V.2).
2. cf. Augustine, *In Ioann.* ev. tract. 26:18 (NPNF, 1st ser., 7.173).
3. LCC, 106 (VI.1). Radbert distinguishes venial and mortal sin.

27

might be a member in his body, and he is a temple of the Holy Spirit.[4]

The elements nourish, invigorate, and prepare him "for things immortal and eternal."[5] In the elements "eternity" and "participation in Christ" is granted to men.[6] Those who eat the elements "in worthy fashion will never see death through all eternity."[7] To unbelievers, nothing miraculous is offered.[8] To believers, "nothing more miraculous" and "nothing richer in this life" is offered.[9]

DESCRIPTION OF THE REQUISITE WORTHINESS—TO PARTAKE BY FAITH

Radbert sees power in the sacrament, which can only be sufficiently imbibed by faith.[10] Radbert's argument is that "we must believe the change has taken place even though we cannot see it, and that we shall find to our profit that it has."[11] Faith and knowledge nurture each other according to Radbert and communicants should not be "ignorant or unaware what in it pertains to faith and what to knowledge."[12] If understanding does not accompany faith, "what has been produced for our cure should end in ruin for those who receive it."[13]

---

4. LCC, 105 (V.3).
5. LCC, 100 (III.3).
6. LCC, 95 (I.4).
7. LCC, 94–95 (I.4).
8. LCC, 95 (I.4).
9. LCC, 95 (I.4).
10. LCC, 106 (VI. 2).
11. Bromiley, *Historical Theology: An Introduction*, 162.
12. LCC (II.1–2).
13. LCC (II.1–2).

THE RESULT OF UNWORTHY PARTAKING OF THE ELEMENTS

However, the power of the sacrament is withdrawn from the one who eats without discerning that the consecrated elements are Christ's body and blood.[14] Since Christ's incarnated body is open to examination by the senses, but only by faith is the incarnation discerned, so the communicant must discern the elements by faith, even though the elements are open to examination by the senses:

> ... but if the truth behind the figure in the Eucharist is the incarnation body, which lies in the sensory sphere, then why should the demand be made for faith in the change in order that it may be discerned?[15]

Radbert distinguishes the spiritual and unspiritual communicant: "one man spiritually eats the flesh of Christ" while "another man does not." The unspiritual communicant does not receive flesh and blood "of value, but judgment," not understanding "anything other than what he feels with his lips." The power of the sacrament applied to the spiritual observer is "withdrawn from him" because "he makes a bad use of something good."[16] To partake without understanding the miraculous transformation and without examining whether one is fit to partake[17] is to be "doubly condemned" because of "presumption."[18] This compares to Chrysostom's view when he says, "and you do this when you come to the table of Christ, on that very day when you are considered worthy to touch His flesh with your tongue. Therefore, lest these things happen, purify your right hand, your tongue, your lips, those things which are the entryway through which Christ comes to us. We are the temple of Christ, and therefore we kiss

---

14. LCC, 106 (VI.2).
15. Bromiley, *Historical Theology: An Introduction*, 162.
16. LCC, 106 (VI.2).
17. Aulen, *Eucharist and Sacrifice*, 55.
18. LCC, 106 (VI.2).

the entrance of this temple."[19] One spiritually consumes Christ, but the one who does not discern the elements brings judgment upon himself,[20] committing a venial sin.[21] The "sinner" according to Radbert does not consume elements "of value."[22]

The closing anecdote to Radbert's work is a stern warning against unworthy partaking.[23] According to Radbert, Syrus, martyred at Milan in the reign of Nero, celebrated the Supper in the church of the martyrs Gervasius and Protasius.[24] An unbelieving Jew, "put up by an evil spirit," took the elements vainly with intent of spitting them out upon a dunghill. But God scoffed at the scoffers:

> [S]truck with fitting punishment, he began loudly to cry out, but his words were unintelligible . . . . He attempted to shut his lips but could not; he tried to speak but his stiff tongue would not function properly and, as if he were carrying a burning dart in his mouth, he was tortured with mighty pain. The whole church rang with the clamor of his bawling. . . . The one presiding over the rite uttered before the throng: Soul who are without faith and full of perfidy, why have you fulfilled the plan of the wicked adversary to make you think the body of Christ

---

19. Chrysostom, *Homilia 27* in 1 *ad Cornithios*. In the same vein, Hilary warns that "we must not speak of the things of God in a human or secular fashion, nor must we allow our perversity to twist the purity of the heavenly words into an alien and irreverent meaning by a violent and improper predication." Hilary quoted in MPL, 10.247.

20. LCC, 106 (VI.2).

21. Supra note 113 (VI.1).

22. LCC, 106 (VI.2).

23. cf. Augustine in *Contra Donatistas*, Bk. 3, ch. 14: "When we are dealing with the completeness and sanctity of the sacrament, there is no difference as to what a person believes or what faith he who receives the sacrament is imbued; there is a very great difference as to the matter of his salvation, but as to the question of the sacrament there is no difference at all. For it can happen that a man possesses the complete sacrament and yet has a perverse faith. Further, as Augustine states in Bk. 7, ch. 33 "Salvation belongs alone to those who are good, but the sacraments are given to the good and bad alike."

24. Ambrose, *Epist.* 22; Augustine *Conf.* 9.7; Augustine, *Act Sactorum*, June, 3.817–847.

very cheap? Look, what secret enticer has seduced you, poor man, to make you do this has been shown to all his faithful by divine power.[25]

According to Syrus, the prophecy of Simeon in Luke 2:34,[26] that the Word is danger and destruction to the faithless, was fulfilled. Syrus took the mystery of the holy Eucharist from the "sacrilegious mouth," saying, "Look new, unbeliever, you have been freed. From now on take care not to do anything similar or to repeat this, lest something worse happen to you."[27] When the Jew confessed and desired to have the water of sacred baptism, Syrus prayed, "O God the omnipotent Father to thee I give thanks, who has not disdained to correct Jewish treachery but convertest it to faith in the only-begotten Son in full piety."

Anecdotes similar to the conversion of the Jew are prolific during the Eucharistic controversy in the ninth century. A flurry of tales of miraculous events, such as the appearance of blood, proliferated in the wake of Radbert's ultra-realism.[28] These bizarre tales circulating at the time may have prompted Charles' inquiry to Ratramn.

---

25. LCC, 107, (VI.3).

26. The biblical reference in the LCC edition is Luke 2:25, probably incorrect. Luke 2:34 better fits Radbert's point in context.

27. LCC, 107, (VI.3).

28. Francis Clark, *Eucharistic Sacrifice and the Reformation* (Westminster, MD.: The Newman Press, 1960), 420–21.

Chapter 4

RATRAMN'S VIEW OF THE ELEMENTS IN THE EUCHARIST

An Introduction to Ratramn's View

WHAT ARE THE ISSUES?

The Motive and Challenge of Ratramn's Treatise

Ratramn's burden is that the subjects under Charles' hegemony should not hold "variant opinions" on a matter as important as Christ's body, "upon which . . . the whole of Christian redemption rests."[1] Ratramn, appreciating the command of 1 Corinthians 1:10, makes a plea for unanimity.[2] Ratramn thinks that the event of transformation is "incomprehensible" and "inestimable."[3] "One must not inquire by what method this could be done but exercise

---

1. LCC, 118. For Moule's helpful abridgment of Ratramn's work, see Ridley, *A Brief Declaration of the Lord's Supper*, Appendix II, 223–48.
2. LCC, 118.
3. LCC, 125.

the faith that it was done."[4] Ratramn attempts to prove that those, like Radbert, who think the transformation occurs in truth and not in a figure are "out of harmony with the writings of the holy fathers."[5] Accordingly, Ratramn denies his arguments derive from his own exegesis, but rather he appeals to the "holy fathers' " authority.[6]

The Issue Addressed in Ratramn's Treatise

The issue Ratramn addresses is "what actually goes into the mouth of communicant?" Ratramn sets out to decide whether the elements become the body and blood of Christ in a mystery or in physical composition.[7] More specifically, under the second option, does the physical composition alter so that it acquires "some hidden element" or does physical composition alter to become that actual body born of Mary only maintaining its original appearance?[8] Ratramn clarifies the issue by the choice of two options: either the elements are a "naked manifestation of truth" or they are the figure of mystery—that is, "one thing which appears to bodily sense and another which faith beholds."[9]

RATRAMN'S THESIS

Ratramn's thesis is that the elements in communion maintain similar visible appearance but spiritually "come to be Christ's body." Outwardly, the form and substance of the elements remain identical. Inwardly, God reveals Christ's body in the elements to

---

4. LCC, 125.
5. LCC, 32–96.
6. LCC, 119.
7. LCC, 119.
8. LCC, 119.
9. LCC, 2; Bromiley, *Historical Theology: An Introduction*, 162.

the communicant, who "behold, receive, and consume" Christ's body spiritually by faith.[10]

Augustine confirms that "the bread which is used for the purpose of receiving the sacrament is consumed."[11] With regard to this physical eating of the substance of the bread, because it is evident, known, and manifest to our senses and our experience, it is unnecessary to say more. But in light of this union, the body of Christ is predicated of that bread which is eaten physically, so that according to the words of Christ those who eat it are rightly and properly said to be eating not only the bread but also the body of Christ. Ratramn expounds an Augustinian realism—after the words of consecration, the bread and wine no longer exist because they have become a new reality, the spiritual body and blood of Christ.[12] Gustaf Aulen defines realism appropriately:

> What happens through the real presence in bread and wine is that the living Christ actualized his eternally valid sacrifice and makes it into an effectively present reality.[13]

Ratramn concedes that to the senses the bread and wine remain bread and wine, but "after the mystical consecration" they are viewed by faith to be the body and blood of Christ.[14] Therefore, to Ratramn, "what are seen and what are believed are not the same."[15]

Ratramn denies, however, that Christ's body is visibly and tangibly in the Eucharist. Ratramn explains that the reality of the Eucharist is a hidden reality in the same fashion as a figure of speech hides its real referent. Accordingly, Ratramn argues that the presence and immolation of Christ must be apprehended spiritually, not literally.[16] Augustine's letter to Boniface in 408 sparked

---

10. LCC, 120.
11. Augustine, De Trinitate, Bk. 5, ch. 10, MPL 42:918.
12. Fahey, *The Eucharistic Teaching of Ratramn of Corbie*, 164.
13. Aulen, *Eucharist and Sacrifice*, 94.
14. LCC, 121; cf. Cyril of Jerusalem, Catechism 4.
15. LCC, 121; cf. Cyril of Jerusalem, Catechism 4.
16. cf. Fahey, *The Eucharistic Teaching of Corbie*, 163. Compare this also

centuries of discussion of the so-called immolation of Christ: "Was not Christ immolated but once, in his own person? And yet not only every year in the Paschal liturgy but every day he is immolated sacramentally for the people; and if one were asked whether he is now immolated, one would reply without falsehood that he is."[17] Gregory added to this conversation his view that Christ, "who 'rising from the dead dieth now no more, death shall no more have dominion over him,' nevertheless is immolated for us again in this mystery of the sacred oblation, while living always, untouchable by death or harm."[18] Alger's summary encapsulates the view of immolation through a consensus of early medieval theologians: "the immolation of Chrst at the altar is so called not because Christ is again killed, but his true immolation therein represented works the same effects now at the altar that it worked then on the cross."[19] And, before his death in 1095, Guitmond of Aversa tersely summed up the traditional doctrine of immolation by stating, "When we say, 'Christ is immolated,' in the celebration of the rite of the Lord's body, no one ought to take this literally, according to a carnal interpretation. For Christ died once and 'dieth now no more, death shall no more have dominion over him.' But when in celebrating Mass we commemorate his passion, he is symbolized as having died formerly for us."[20] Ratramn's phraseology attributes

---

to Augustine in *Contra adversarium legis et prophetiarum*, Bk. 2, ch. 9, who states "we, however, take into our believing hearts and mouths the Mediator between God and man, the man Jesus Christ with His flesh given us to eat and His blood given us to drink." Above all, Augustine's letter to Boniface inserted the language of immolation into medieval theology, repeated by Radbertus (d. 851), Ratramnus (d. 868), Lanfrac of Canterbury (d. 1089), Alger of Liege (d. 1130), Abelard (d. 1142), and William of St. Theirry (d. 1150). Clark, *Eucharistic Sacrifice and the Reformation*, 405.

17. Augustine, *Epistola* 98, 9; P.L. XXXIII, col. 363.

18. Gregory, *Dialogues*, Book IV, chap. 58, section 9; Clark, *Eucharistic Sacrifice and the Reformation*, 405.

19. Alger, *De sacramentis*, lib. I, cap. 16; P.L. CLXXX, col. 786.

20. Guitmond, *De corporis et sanguinis Christi vertitate in Eucharistia*, book I; P. L. CLXXX, col. 786. "Hence if anyone should say that the celebration of the rite of the Lord's body is the Lord's passion, understanding this in a carnal sense, we will bid him be gone. For this celebration of this rite is not a

"to the Eucharist effects which could be attained only by a spiritual entity."[21]

RATRAMN'S DEFINITION OF HIS TERMS

Ratramn's vocabulary of the Eucharistic terms includes "eucharist," "*bona gratia*," "sacrament," "mystery," "making," "sacrifice," "figure," and "truth." Ratramn approves of both the Greek designation *eucharisto* (thanksgiving) and the Latin designation *bona gratia* (good grace).[22] According to Ratramn, a sacrament involves elements which "under cover of corporeal objects the divine power secretly dispenses the salvation of those who receive it by faith."[23] Ratramn agrees with Isidore of Seville that Baptism and the Lord's Supper are "called sacraments from powers both secret and holy."[24] Also in agreement with Isidore, Ratramn believes the bread:

> is transferred into the body of Christ while it is being consecrated. So also the wine . . . is made the blood of Christ through the consecration of the divine mystery—not visibly, of course, but as this doctor says, working invisibly through the Spirit of God.[25]

Ratramn also cites approvingly the use of the term "sacrifice" by Isidore: "Sacrifice is so called from *sacra* and *fieri*, 'that which is made holy,' because it is consecrated by mystical prayer

---

passion of the Lord, but the symbolic communication of the passion formerly accomplished."

21. Fahey, *The Eucharistic Teaching of Ratramn of Corbie*, 164.
22. LCC, 130.
23. LCC, 132; Isidore, *Etym.* 6.19.39f.
24. Guitmond, *De corporis et sanguinis Christi vertitate in Eucharistia*, book I; P. L. CLXXX, col. 786. "Hence if anyone should say that the celebration of the rite of the Lord's body is the Lord's passion, understanding this in a carnal sense, we will bid him be gone. For this celebration of this rite is not a passion of the Lord, but the symbolic communication of the passion formerly accomplished."
25. Fahey, *The Eucharistic Teaching of Ratramn of Corbie*, 164. LCC, 131.

to commemorate the Lord's suffering in our behalf."[26] Echoing Augustine, Ratramn agrees the one presiding over the Supper does not lie when he says that Christ is sacrificed.[27] Ratramn explains that designating the Supper a "sacrifice" is metonymical, however. Modern-day critic J.I. Packer's view of this is "Since, on the one hand, Christ's own sacrifice is a perfect act of obedience to the will of God by the last Adam, the second representative Man, the archetype and head of recreated humanity; and since, on the other hand, Christians are 'members of his body, of his flesh, and of his bones' (Eph. 5:30), forming with him a single complex unity, 'Christ mystical' (cf. 1 Cor. 12:12); therefore the Church's self-offering, made in imitation of Christ's, is in the sight of God organically one with it."[28] Ridley, also influenced by Ratramn, agreed that, "Christ Himself constantly presents them to God 'a living sacrifice,' as they present themselves. . . . [T]hey present to God . . . not only themselves as a sacrifice, but Him; not only their own sacrifice, but His also."[29]

---

26. LCC, 130.

LCC, 130; Isidore of Seveille, Etymologiae sive origines.

27. LCC, 132; Isidore, *Etym.* 6.19.39f.

Augustine, *Epist.* 98.9 (formerly 23.9) *ad Banifatium episcopum* (MPL 33.359-364, quotation in coll. 363 f. =CSEL 34.520-533, quotation on pp. 530 f., tr. NPNF, 1st scr., 1.409).

28. Isidore, *Etym.* 6.19.42.

J.I. Packer, *Introduction: Lambeth, 1958*, in *Eucharistic Sacrifice: The Addresses Given at the Oxford Conference of Evangelical Churchmen* (London: Church Book Room Press, 1962), 6. Packer goes on to say, "The self-oblation of Christ mystical is assimilated to that of Christ personal in such a sense that the former is seen as no more, and no less, than an extension, and hence an aspect, of the latter. The sacrifice of Christ, and of all faithful persons who sacrifice themselves to God in Him, is one sacrifice."

29. Ridley, *A Brief Declaration of the Lord's Supper*, 6-7. Interacting with the "great heap of patristic authors who call communion a sacrifice, Cranmer responds ". . . they call it not a sacrifice for sin, because that it taketh away our sin, which is taken away only by the death of Christ, but because the holy communion was ordained of Christ to put us in remembrance of that sacrifice made by him on the cross; for that cause it beareth the same of that sacrifice, as St. Augustine . . . saith: 'That which men call a sacrifice is a representation of the true sacrifice.'" Thomas Cranmer, *On the Lord's Supper*, Parker Society, 346.

Ratramn calls the elements "representations"[30] or "figures" of the actual body and blood of Christ.[31] To Ratramn, a 'figure' is a metaphor standing for its referent. It is "an overshadowing that reveals its intent under some sort of veil." A figure "says one thing and hints at another."[32] For instance, "bread" in the Lord's Prayer, to Ratramn, represents the Word (*cf.* Luke 11:3). Similarly, "living bread" in John 6:41 represents Christ, as does the "vine" in John 15:5. Ratramn echoes Augustine who explains John 6:52–53 as a non-literal command because otherwise, "this would order a shameful crime." Rather, the statement is a "figure, enjoining that we should have a share in the Lord's suffering, and that we should faithfully remember that for us his flesh was crucified and wounded."[33]

Interpreting Ratramn's Use of the Term "Figure"

In Ratramn's view, the term "figure" has different meanings. It is equivalent to metaphor when he is speaking of a discourse or of a word; it indicates the real and sensible veil of a reality and of an invisible virtue really contained when it is used with reference to a sacrament; and it is the memory and the record of a real event (the sacrifice of the cross) when it refers to the celebration of the Eucharistic sacrifice.[34] Gliozzo actually sees different referents for the term "figure." "Figure" may stand for the word or message of

---

30. cf. Aquinas, who described the elements as representations: "Symbolically, no doubt, in the breaking of the bread and the outpouring of the wine, and in the separate consecration of the bread and of the wine, there is represented the violation of Christ's body and the outpouring of his blood . . ." Aquinas quoted in Charles Gore, *The Body of Christ: An Inquiry into the Institution and Doctrine of Holy Communion* (London: John Murray, 1901), 174.

31. LCC, 130.

32. LCC.

33. Augustine, *De doctr.* Chr. 3.16.24 (MPL 34.74–75, tr. NPNF, 1st serm., 2.563).

34. Gliozzo, 114.

the Eucharist, the physical elements representing the actual body and blood, and the memory or record of the sacrifice of the cross.[35]

Truth, however, is a "representation of clear facts ... uttered in pure and open and ... natural meanings."[36] Veritas in Ratramn's work denotes physical truth, not philosophical truth.[37] Accordingly, the consecrated elements are not the historical body of Jesus "in truth" but "in a figure." Ratramn then illustrates that Christ was not "in truth" but "in a figure" described as a "rock" and "manna" from 1 Corinthians 10 and John 6, respectively.[38]

Ratramn also refers to the Eucharist by metonymy. Just as the Lord's Day is called "the Pascha" and "the Lord's resurrection," so Ratramn calls the sacrament of the body and blood of Christ, "the body and blood" of Christ.[39] Ratramn grounds his use of metonymy on the theology of representation involved in the Eucharist. Since the elements are representations of this resemblance, they derive their names from those things of which they are sacraments. Therefore, as in some manner "the sacrament of Christ's body is Christ's body, the sacrament of Christ's blood is Christ's blood, so the sacrament of faith is faith."[40] Further, Sedulius Scottus (?848–858) repeats the traditional definition of the noun inherited from Donatus and Priscian, "agreeing that nouns signify things, that they signify them both commonly and properly, and that appellatives can refer to traits both generic and specific, while proper nouns denote only the substance and qualities of individuals. Sedulius takes a step forward, however as the first Carolingian grammarian to draw a clear distinction between words, their referents, and their meanings. He states, "The word signifying is one thing; the things signified are another; and the signification is still

---

35. Gliozzo, 114.
36. Bromiley, *Historical Theology: An Introduction*, 162.
37. LCC, 118.
38. LCC, 20–31.
39. LCC, 129.
40. Augustine, *Epist.* 98.9 (formerly 23.9) *ad Banifatium episcopum* (MPL 33.359–364, quotation in coll. 363 f. =CSEL 34.520–533, quotation on page 530 f., tr. NPNF, 1st scr., 1.409).

another. For the signification is the idea of some thing expressly by the articulate voice."[41] Similarly, Ratramn echoes Augustine who taught that the one presiding over the Supper does not lie when he says that Christ is sacrificed.[42] Ratramn sees the statement as a metonymy of the commemoration substituted for the historical event.

A PRÉCIS OF RATRAMN'S THEOLOGY

Fahey correctly distills Ratramn's thinking about the Eucharist into six charged but accurate propositions:

> The appearance and constitutive elements of the two Bodies are different.
> The Eucharistic Body represents the Church while the historical Body did not.
> The historical Body is completely incorruptible, but the Body upon the altar has the appearances of changeable bread.
> The two Bodies cannot be defined in the same way.
> The Liturgy of the Mass makes a clear distinction between them.
> Calvary was a real sacrifice while the Mass is but a memorial. Saint Augustine marks off the sacraments from the realities which they represent.

The *sine qua non* of Ratramn's theology of the Eucharist is summarily comprehended in the following syllogism:

Things that are different are not identical.

The Eucharistic flesh and blood differ from the flesh and blood which hung upon Calvary.

Therefore, they are not the same.[43]

---

41. Fahey, *The Eucharistic Teaching of Ratramn of Corbie*, 47 (Aliud est enim vox signigicans, aliun significata, aliud est significatio; significatio enim est alicuius rei articulata voce expressa notitio).

42. Augustine, *Epist.* 98.9 (formerly 23.9) *ad Banifatium episcopum* (MPL 33.359–364, quotation in coll. 363 f. =CSEL 34.520–533, quotation on page 530 f., tr. NPNF, 1st scr., 1.409).

43. Fahey, *The Eucharistic Teaching of Ratramn of Corbie*, 46.

RATRAMN'S VIEW OF THE ELEMENTS IN THE EUCHARIST

Ratramn here posits a distinction between the Eucharistic elements and the historical body of Christ.[44]

Although the elements and their referents are not the same, the symbolism of the elements involves a spiritual dynamic. As A.J. MacDonold concludes, Ratramn sees the symbolism not as stark objects of memorial but as active agents of spiritual experience:

> The symbolism of the sacrament is dynamic. It produces in the recipient the effect of the body of Christ. It contains the virtue or power of the Word, an inward latent power, the effectiveness of His body, for life is in the bread, and this is the body of Christ.[45]

The symbolic value of the elements in Ratramn's thinking is infinite, imparting immortality to the recipients, in the form of grace and virtue.[46] But the efficacy of the elements does not derive from their transformation into the historical body of Christ. Their efficacy derives from God himself. This compares to Calvin's view of the efficacy of the elements. Calvin in the Formula of Agreement states "that the body of Christ is distributed efficaciously, but not naturally; according to its power, but not according to its substance."[47] Similarly, in the Defense of the Agreement he reiterates, "the body of Christ is given to us and it nourishes us to the extent that while remaining in heaven He descends to us with His power." He pours out the life-giving power of His flesh upon us and we are nourished through its rays no less than by the vital warmth of the sun. "The power and ability of giving life cannot properly be called something that is separated from its substance."[48]

---

44. Ibid., 98.

45. A.J. Macdonald, *Berengar and the Reform of Sacramental Doctrine* (London: Longmans, Green and Co., 1930), 239ff.

46. Macdonald, *Berengar and the Reform of Sacramental Doctrine*, 239ff.

47. Aulen, *Eucharist and Sacrifice*, 42.

48. Aulen, *Eucharist and Sacrifice*, 42.

Chapter 5

RATRAMN'S THEOLOGY OF TRANSFORMATION

What Happens to the Elements?

THE ACT OF TRANSFORMATION—HOW ARE THE ELEMENTS TRANSFORMED?

The Crux—Change Only in the Spiritual Dimension

The crux of Ratramn's Eucharistic theology is his view of transformation of the elements. In general, Ratramn sees only three kinds of change:

For every change is brought either from that which it is not to that which it is, or from that which it is to that which it is not, or from that which it is to that which it is.[1]

However, the Eucharist does not involve change "from what is being to what is not being," that is, a "birth."[2] Ratramn explains that the substance of the elements remains the same: "according to

---

1. cf. Ps.-Augustine, *Categoriae decem ex Aristotele decerptae* 21 (MPL 32.1439A).
2. LCC, 121.

the truth the appearance of the creature which formerly existed is recognized to have remained."[3]

While Ratramn agrees that to the senses the elements remain bread and wine, he argues that "after the mystical consecration" they are viewed by faith to be the body and blood of Christ.[4] The transition is not one of variance of quality, such as that which would be involved in transition for an object which can change in color from black from white. Rather, one does not apprehend anything to have altered "in either touch or color or smell."[5] Some "change for the better," has taken place, not in a corporeal but a spiritual sense. Figuratively, "under cover of the corporeal bread and of the corporeal wine Christ's spiritual body and spiritual blood do exist."[6] Christ is truly in the sacrament, but not present in a manner visible to the eyes of the body.[7]

Analogs of Spiritual Change

Through a variety of analogs—baptism, the cloud and parted sea, as well as the manna and split rock—Ratramn communicates the nature of spiritual change. As the waters of baptism[8] purify "not only bodies but also souls, and it removes spiritual filth by means

---

3. LCC, 121; cf. Ambrose, *De sacram.* 2.5, 66 Botte: <Spiritus Sanctus> quasi columba.

4. LCC, 121; cf. Cyril of Jerusalem, *Catechism* 4.

5. LCC, 122.

6. LCC, 122–23.

7. Gonzalez, A History *of Christian Thought: From Augustine to the Eve of the Reformation*, 119.

8. Thomas M. Parker, review of *Ratramnus: De Corpero et Sanguine Domini: Texte original et notive bibliiogaphique. Edition renouvelee par J.N. Bakuizen van den Brink*. (Amsterdam, London: North Holland Publishing Company, 1974) *Journal of Theological Studies*, n.s., 29:245-47 (April 1978): 246. Ratramn believed that the sacramental power of the baptismal water derives from its prior consecration by a priest (XVII)—an application of 'conversion theology' to baptism which (as in some Eastern Fathers and even in Tertullian) teaches a kind of real presence of the Holy Ghost in the water, a realism which has never been accepted by the majority of Christian theologians.

of spiritual power," so the elements possess spiritual power to affect the communicant.[9] The "sea and cloud granted the purification and sanctification not with respect to what they were as body, but they contained the sanctification of the Holy Spirit with respect to that they were invisibly."[10] To the physical senses, the visible form appeared as sea and a cloud "in truth," but from "within spiritual power shone forth, which appeared not to the eyes."[11]

Although the manna and the water flowing from the rock were corporeal, Paul identifies the manna and water as spiritual food and drink.[12] The manna and water nourished the souls of people because the "power of the spiritual word inhered in these bodily substances."[13] Ratramn sees the spiritual food and drink in the wilderness as "the same" as the spiritual food and drink of the Lord's Supper.[14] Ratramn understands the designation "angels' food" not as the corporeal nourishment of angels, but spiritual nourishment of both angels and believers by the power of the spiritual Word.[15]

Ratramn paraphrases Christ's words in John 6:52–53 interpretively, explaining by apostrophe what Christ said:

> . . . you will understand that my flesh does not have to be eaten by believers, as men without faith suppose, but the bread and wine, by the mystery truly changed into the substance of my body and blood, must be taken by believers.[16]

In sum, through a spiritual dimension believers may imbibe Christ by faith by partaking of the elements.

9. LCC, 131.
10. LCC, 124.
11. LCC, 124.
12. LCC, 124.
13. LCC, 124.
14. LCC, 124.
15. LCC, 126.
16. LCC, 127.

THE RESULT OF TRANSFORMATION—TO WHAT ARE THE ELEMENTS TRANSFORMED?

Transformed by the "agency of the divine Spirit," who works by "invisible power,"[17] the resultant elements are not two substances of which one is physical and the other spiritual. The elements are the same substance, but Ratramn draws a distinction in their composition from the perspective of the viewer. From the conventional point of view, the elements have the appearance of bread and wine; from the spiritual point of view, the elements are the body and blood of Christ.[18]

The elements, transformed in the consecration, possess a secret and hidden character—they are mysterious in that they differ in outward and inward dimensions. Their outward form signifies what they are under the original creation; their inward[19] and invisible dimension is a newly created entity.[20] Ratramn denies expressly that the elements are transformed into the "very body which was born of Mary, suffered, died, and was buried, and which sits on the right hand of the Father." The physical makeup of the elements remains the same: "for with respect to the substance of things created, what they had been before consecration, that they afterward are."[21] Ratramn frames the debate with a rhetorical question:

> What is taken in bodily form, what the teeth press into, what is swallowed by the gullet, what is taken into the cavern of the stomach, does not provide the substance of eternal life, does it?

---

17. LCC, 131.
18. LCC, 123.
19. cf. Gregory, *Homilia paschali*, 22: "you will learn what the blood of the Lamb is not by hearing but by drinking. This blood is placed above each doorpost when it is drunk not only with our bodily mouth but also with the mouth of the heart."
20. cf. LCC, 132 (47).
21. LCC, 133.

According to Ratramn, the corruptible physical elements cannot bestow the "boon of never dying."[22]

Ratramn explains that "what lies close to corruption has no power to bestow eternity."[23] But, despite the corruptible dimension of the elements, life in the elements is present, but can not be seen with the naked eye—only the eyes of faith.[24] "Therefore, what faith sees, what feeds the soul, what provides the substance of eternal life, has been changed inwardly by the mighty power of the Holy Spirit."[25] However, in the absence of faith, the elements cannot be spiritually nourishing to the communicant because faith is required to spiritually perceive. Without spiritual perception, there can be no spiritual consumption. Therefore, Ratramn underscores the necessity of faith as a conduit to receive benefit: "Now, however, because faith sees all that is, and the eye of flesh perceives nothing, understand that it is not in appearance but in power that Christ's body and blood are what they appear to be."[26] By faith, the communicant perceives that Christ is not present "in truth," but "figuratively." Ratram does not deny the real presence of Christ's body in the elements because that which exists figuratively can be perceived spiritually. What exists in truth can be perceived only externally.[27] But, that which exists in truth is not more real than that which exists in a figure.[28]

Ratramn, with Anselm, holds that a creative act takes place. Ratramn cites Anselm's argument from greater to the lessor: Cannot the word of Christ, which was able to make from nothing that which was not, change the things that are into what they were

---

22. LCC, 132–33.

23. LCC, 133.

24. cf. LCC, 133.

25. LCC, 133.

26. LCC, 134.

27. Gonzalez, *A History of Christian Thought: From Augustine to the Eve of the Reformation*, 118.

28. Gonzalez, *A History of Christian Thought: From Augustine to the Eve of the Reformation*, 119.

not? Is it not a greater act to give new things than to change their natures?[29]

Ratramn agrees with Anselm that "the body of Christ is the body of the divine Spirit." Ratramn understands Anselm to mean that the:

> [d]ivine Spirit exists as nothing which is corporeal, nothing corruptible, nothing capable of being touched. But this body which is celebrated in the church with respect to its visible appearance is both corruptible and capable of being touched.[30]

In support, Ratramn cites Jerome's commentary on Ephesians 1:7 where the flesh and blood[31] of Christ are understood in a spiritual/divine sense and a physical sense.[32] Ratramn presupposes that some change has taken place. If it is impossible that no physical change has taken place, and also that no visible change has taken place, then some "spiritual change" must have taken place.[33] If nothing has happened to alter the elements, in Ratramn's thinking, the elements can not be "Christ's body and blood."

Although Ratramn agrees that a creative act takes place, he does not equate the transformed elements with the actual body of Christ:

> They are therefore not the same. For that flesh which was crucified was made from the flesh of the Virgin. . . . But the spiritual flesh which spiritually feeds the people

29. Ambrose, *De myst.* 9.52, p. 125 Botte = MPL 16:424A.

30. LCC, 136.

31. LCC, 139. In relation to the blood, Ratramn believes that the mixing of the wine with the water is prescribed, the one not allowed to be served without the other. The water, according to Ratramn, represents the people. Ratramn explains that the people cannot exist without Christ, and Christ cannot exist without the people. Ratramn illustrates as the head cannot exist without the body, the body cannot exist without the head. "Whatever is meant in the water concerning the body of the people is accepted spiritually." cf. F.J. Dolger, *Der helige Tisch in den antiken Religionen und im Christentum* (Munster I. W., 2d ed., 1928), 2.491–496; Ambrose, De virg. 3.5.22.

32. Jerome, *In Eph.* 1:7 (MPL 26.481).

33. LCC, 122.

who believe, consists with respect to the appearance it outwardly bears, of grains of flour molded by the hand of an artisan, joined together without sinews and bones, having no characteristic variation of parts, animated by no rational substance, unable to move of its own accord, for whatever in it furnishes the substance of life is of spiritual might, invisible in efficacy, and divine power.[34]

Of necessity, therefore, Christ's body must also not be understood corporeally but spiritually.[35]

Ratramn explains that a transformation may be from non-being to being, or from one form of being to another. Radbert denies any transformation in being per se,[36] because "nothing is seen to have changed"[37]—"it is nothing but what it was before."[38] At the same time however, Ratramn argues that the element "is another thing because the bread is made the body of Christ."[39] Ratramn reasons that either the elements are not Christ's body and blood or that they have been "changed in some respect other than the bodily one."[40] Therefore, the change is a spiritual and figurative one.[41] The element in the Supper "exhibits one thing to human sense and proclaims another thing inwardly to the minds of the faithful." Although the senses perceive one thing, another reality is perceived by the "gaze of the believing soul." Therefore, "in a figurative sense," the elements are the body and blood of Christ."[42] Ratramn never denies the reality of Christ's presence in

---

34. LCC, 138.
35. LCC, 139.
36. LCC, 12–13.
37. LCC, 1–15.
38. LCC, 13.
39. LCC, 13; Bromiley, *Historical Theology: An Introduction*, 163.
40. LCC, 15; Bromiley, *Historical Theology: An Introduction*, 164.
41. LCC, 16; Bromiley, *Historical Theology: An Introduction*, 164.
42. LCC, 9–10; Bromiley, *Historical Theology: An Introduction*, 162.

RATRAMN'S THEOLOGY OF TRANSFORMATION

the Eucharist.[43] Rather his work discounts the crass literalism of a Capharnaitic, ultra-realist conception of the Eucharist.[44]

But Ratramn underscores the distinction in the physical/corruptible dimension and spiritual/eternal dimension comprising the elements, saying "it is one thing, however, which is outwardly done, but another which through faith is believed."[45] The contrast between the physical and spiritual dimensions is a denial of transubstantiation. Gonzalez distills Ratramn's view against the ubiquity of Christ's body:

> The body of Christ which is present in the eucharist is not the same body of Christ which was born of Mary and hung from the cross, for the latter, which is presently at the right hand of the Father, is visible, and in the eucharist is only spiritual, and it is spiritually that the believer partakes in it. This does not mean that Ratramnus understands communion as a mere act of remembrance. On the contrary, Christ is truly present in the elements, but in a spiritual manner, not accessible to the senses of the flesh.[46]

---

43. Fahey, The *Eucharistic Teaching of Ratramn of Corbie*, 164.

44. Ibid., 164.

45. LCC, 140.

46. Gonzalez, *A History of Christian Thought: From Augustine to the Eve of the Reformation*, 119. Regarding Ratramn's use of the term substantia, Thomas Parker concludes: "although Ratramn denies, as against what he takes to be the teaching of Paschasius, any change of what he describes as 'Substance' in the consecrated elements and appears to contradict St. Ambrose—'Nam secundum creaturarum stubstantiam, quod fuerent ante consecrationem, hoc et postea conistunt' (ch. LIV)—it would be dangerous to assume that he is using susbtantia in its strict Aristotelian sense, as a schoolman would have done. He was, no doubt, one of those who, like Augustine in some passages (although not in others), looked at the Eucharistic elements as primarily symbols, but we must remember that in his day 'Symbol' and cognate terms did not, as they do now, denote a contrast with reality." Thomas M. Parker, review of *Ratramnus: De Corpero et Sanguine Domini: Texte original et notive bibliiogaphique. Edition renouvelee par J.N. Bakuizen van den Brink.* (Amsterdam, London: North Holland Publishing Company, 1974) *Journal of Theological Studies*, n.s., 29:245-47 (April 1978): 246.

Ratramn quotes Augustine in support his own argument. In a similar vein, Augustine distinguishes between the sacrament proper and its spiritual power: "... the sacrament is one thing and the power of the sacrament is another."[47] Augustine analogizes the elements of the sacrament to the manna in the wilderness. Moses, Aaron, and Phinehas, remarks Augustine, did not die because "they understood the visible food spiritually, they hungered spiritually, they tasted spiritually, so that they might be satisfied spiritually."[48] Augustine echoes that the one who spiritually benefits from the sacrament is the one who "eats it within, not outside, who eats it in his heart, not who crushes it with his teeth."[49] The elements themselves, therefore, are "as a figure or memorial of the Lord's death."[50]

---

47. LCC, 140.
48. Augustine, *In Ioann.* evang. tract. 26.11 (MPL 35.1611).
49. Augustine, *In Ioann.* evang. tract. 26.11 (MPL 25.1612).
50. LCC, 101.

Chapter 6

THE NATURE OF TRANSFORMATION

*Is the Act of Transformation
a Repeated Sacrifice by Christ?*

To Ratramn, the celebration of the Lord's Supper is continuous, but the historical event is "once for all," as per Hebrews 7:26–28: "What the Lord Jesus Christ once and for all fulfilled by offering himself, this in memory of his Passion is daily enacted through the celebration of the mysteries."[1] Ratramn does not object to calling the Eucharist a "sacrifice." As one may call the Lord's Day "the resurrection," or call the elements "the body and blood," so Ratramn explains that in the mysteries "the Lord is both sacrificed and suffers since they bear appearance of his death and Passion, of which they are representations."[2] Ratramn substantiates his continuous representation theory from Isidore in the book of *Etymologies*. In this work, Isidore explains that the elements become the body and blood "through the invisible action of God's spirit."[3] But Ratramn's referring to the Eucharist as a "sacrifice" is only a metonymy of the cause substituted for the result.

1. LCC, 130.
2. LCC, 130.
3. Isisore of Seville, *Etymologiae sive origines* 6.19.48 (Lindsay) = MPL

THE EFFECT OF THE TRANSFORMATION—HOW DO COMMUNICANTS RESPOND?

According to Ratramn, the mystery of transformation of the elements began at the Last Passover/First Lord's Supper, even before the Lord had suffered in death.[4] Accordingly, even before he suffered on the cross, Ratramn states Christ "changed the substance of bread and wine into his own body."[5] In the Upper Room, therefore, did communicants first experience the Eucharist in Ratramn's view.

The Objective Effect of the Transformation

In the mystery of transformation, the effect of the elements is "spiritual. It gives life . . ."[6] Although Christ suffered once for all, Ratramn applies 1 Peter 2:21, which says Christ has left us an "example which in the mystery of the Lord's body and blood is daily represented before the believers."[7] The effect of partaking of the elements derives not from the corporeal content but rather from the soul of the participant who is "nourished and quickened by the Word of God."[8] Ratramn quotes Ambrose who affirms "it is the bread of life eternal which supports the substance of our soul."[9] The Lord's body and blood are spiritually received "when faith receives what the eye does not see but what it believes."[10] Ratramn teaches that the elements are "spiritual food spiritually feeding the soul."[11]

82.255 f.
4. LCC, 126.
5. LCC, 126.
6. LCC, 127.
7. LCC, 129.
8. LCC, 137.
9. LCC, 137; Ambrose, De sacram. 5.24, p. 95 Botte = MPL 16.471.
10. LCC, 101.
11. LCC, 101.

The Subjective Response to the Transformation

Ratramn sees the relation of the transformation of the elements and faith. Accordingly, he refutes the view that "nothing spiritual takes place." To him, if "nothing is here received figuratively, but everything is visible in truth, faith does not operate here." Ratramn's proof text is Hebrews 11:1, which says that faith is "the evidence of things not appearing." Since taking the elements without spiritual content is communing only on what is seen and not what is not seen (or believed in), then taking the elements without appreciation of spiritual content is faithless communing.[12]

Ratramn underscores the responsibility of the communicant and says, "whosoever draws near to it knows that he ought to associate himself in His sufferings, of which he awaits the image in the sacred mysteries."[13] The communicant must have faith that something spiritual has taken place.[14] To Ratramn, faith is the perceiving of the invisible.[15]

For Ratramn, Christ is the image of God, and the image of God is mirrored visibly in the Supper.[16] In the Supper, the participant, as an imitator of Christ, dies with him, confessing his belief by the act of tasting.[17] "The Word of God, who is the living bread, refreshes faithful souls that share in it."[18] For exhortation, Ratramn exposits Ambrose who urges participants to "live that daily you may deserve to receive it."[19]

Ratramn parallels spiritual benefit received in the Eucharist with spiritual benefit received in baptism. Although the water is literal in baptism, the water is parallel to the Holy Spirit because

---

12. LCC, 121.
13. LCC, 129.
14. Bromiley, *Historical Theology: An Introduction*, 162.
15. Bromiley, *Historical Theology: An Introduction*, 162.
16. LCC, 129.
17. LCC, 129; cf. Paschasius (MPL 120.1273), who quotes the passage differently.
18. LCC, 130.
19. LCC, 137.

"in its own properties water is corruptible, but in the mystery it is healing power."[20] So, says Ratramn, as water and the Spirit are parallel in baptism, the elements and Christ are parallel in the Eucharist—through which the spiritual communicant experiences "healing power."[21]

---

20. LCC, 17–18; Bromiley, *Historical Theology: An Introduction*, 164.
21. LCC 17–18; Bromiley, *Historical Theology: An Introduction*, 164.

Chapter 7

THE PLACE OF RATRAMN IN THE DIACHRONIC DEVELOPMENT OF THE THEOLOGY OF THE EUCHARIST

SOURCES OF RATRAMN'S THEOLOGY

John F. Fahey concludes correctly that Ratramn turned to Augustine "as faithfully as a compass points to the north."[1] Like Plato and Plotinus, Augustine postulated a world of ideals to explain existence.[2] However, Augustine replaced Plotinus' vague theory of emanations with the Christian concept of creation.[3] An eager of student of Augustine, Ratramn wrote a treatise *On Predestination*, a refutation of Hincmar. Hincmar argued predestination according to foreknowledge of contingent human choice. Ratramn's thoroughly Augustinian work is replete with substantiating quotes of Gregory, Prosper, and Rulgentius. Ratramn explains that the mass of humanity is a mass of perdition, but God chose some to salvation and the remainder to damnation. God, however, does not predestine man to sin, but predestines man to

---

1. Fahey, *The Eucharistic Teaching of Ratramn of Corbie*, 55, fn. 114.
2. Ibid., 150.
3. Ibid., 150.

the condemnation "that flows from the sin in which he is already involved."[4] The paradox of Ratramn's model—spiritual reality without corporal substance—is akin to the Platonic theories which influenced Augustine. Plato explained the derivation of sensible objects from their ideas in two ways: an imitation (mimhsi) and participation (meqexi). Whether objects imitated or participated in the originating idea, Plato's thought and phraseology calculates to preserve the world of ideas inviolate.[5] Fahey sees Ratramn's conception of the reality of Christ's body in the Eucharist as "midway" between Plato's postulations of idea and phenomenon. The dualism between phenomenon and ideas echoes Augustine's distinction of *sacramentum* (mystery and rite) and *res* (historical event).[6] The presence of the body of Christ is real enough to be a phenomenon but remains an idea—hence Augustinians conceive of the body of Christ *ad modum Ideae*.[7]

Ratramn a Milestone in the Diachronic Development of Eucharistic Doctrine

Among the Carolingians, Ratramn, Gottschalk, Raban Maur, Amalry and Florus took their Eucharistic doctrine from Augustine, while Amalry and Florus are unclear whether Christ's historical body composes the Eucharistic condiments.[8]

Berengius of Tours attempted reviving Ratramn and Erigena in the eleventh century. However, Pope Leo IX condemned the popular and even flamboyant Berengius in 1050. At the Council of Tours in 1054, Berengius signed a compromised creed which was drafted by himself and accepted by the papal legate, Hildrebrand. Though, at the rebuttal of Lanfrac, Berengius further capitulated, conceding in 1059 before the Roman Synod that the elements are

---

4. Gonzalez, *A History of Christian Thought: From Augustine to the Eve of the Reformation*, 112–13.
5. Fahey, *The Eucharistic Teaching of Corbie*, 137.
6. Ibid., 164.
7. Ibid., 164–65.
8. Ibid., 164.

the "true body and blood of our Lord Jesus Christ and that these are sensibly handled and broken by the hands of the priests and crushed by the teeth of the faithful, not only sacramentally but in truth."[9] Berengius later conceded, although not so forthrightly, a substantial change in the elements twenty years later in 1079. Lombard concurred, but denied that Christ's body is broken without breaking of the bread. In the decree of the Fourth Lateran Council the development culminated in a decree of transubstantiation:

> The elements are truly contained in the sacrament of the altar under the species of bread and wine, the bread being transubstantiated into the body and the wine into the blood by the power of God.[10]

Aquinas believed that Ratramn denied the real presence of Christ in the elements.[11] But by the time of the Reformation, Ratramn had become a *cause celebre*. Protestants wanted him for a precursor of their own views, and Catholics wanted to claim him either as a witness to the traditional faith or as a long-discredited heretic.[12] Some deniers of real presence hailed him as an ally from the past. Some Catholics found him perfectly orthodox. And even the Lutheran Centuriators of Magdeburg found in him *semina*

---

9. Macy, *The Theologies of the Eucharist in the Early Scholastic Period: A Study of the Salvific Function of the Sacrament according to the Theologians c. 1080–c. 1220*, 36.

10. Bromiley, *Historical Theology: An Introduction*, 283.

11. Thomas Aquinas, *Summa Theologica*, III, q. LXXV, a. 1. Aquinas denies that the substance of the bread and wine remain after consecration. *Summa*, Part 3, Q. 75, Art. 2; Bromiley, *Historical Theology: An Introduction*, 283. He also denies that the original substance of the elements is annihilated. Bromiley, *Historical Theology: An Introduction*, 283–84. Aquinas argues that transformation into visible human flesh and blood would render the element abhorrent, cause infidels to blaspheme, and obviate the need for the faith (Art. 5).

12. Fahey, *The Eucharistic Teaching of Ratramn of Corbie*, 30.

transsubstantionis,[13] the Madgeburg colloquy[14] concluding that Ratramn was, at least in seed form, a transubstantiationist because he used words "commutation" and "conversion." But John Moehler sees Ratramn and Luther[15] in the same vein:

> Luther had then indeed already rejected the doctrine of transubstantiation; but he still continued, with his accustomed coarseness and violence, yet with great acuteness and most brilliant success, to defend against Zuinglius the real presence of Christ in the Eucharist.[16]

Ratramn's work influenced Ridley, convincing him that the medieval view was neither patristic nor biblical.[17] C.W. Dugmore surmises that the *editio princeps* of 1531 or its successor came into Nicholas Ridley's possession in 1532. As bishop of London, Ridley confessed in 1546 that he was "first pulled by the ear" and "first brought from the common error of the Romish Church" by reading Ratramn's work. In the same year, Cranmer[18] confessed that Ridley drew him away from transubstantiation "by sundry persuasions

---

13. Thomas M. Parker, review of *Ratramnus: De Corpero et Sanguine Domini: Texte original et notive bibliiogaphique*. Edition renouvelee par J. N. Bakuizen van den Brink. (Amsterdam, London: North Holland Publishing Company, 1974), Journal of Theological Studies, n.s., 29:245–47 (April 1978), 247.

14. Magdeburg, *Centuriators*, Cens. 9 de doctrina.

15. Compare Formula of Concord: "the whole eucharistic action, but the command and direction of Christ make the bread into his body and the wine into his blood. "When according to his direction and command we say in the eucharist, 'this is my body,' it is his body, not because of our word or power, but because he has instructed us to say and do this and has connected his command and his action with our words." Aulen, *Eucharist and Sacrifice*, 97.

16. John Moehler, *Symbolism, or Explanation of the Doctrinal Differences between Catholics and Protestants*, trans. by James B. Robertson, (3rd ed.; New York: The Catholic Publishing Col, 1894), 244.

17. Gonzalez, *A History of Christian Thought: From Augustine to the Eve of the Reformation*, 298.

18. The Bishop Brooks of Gloucester quipped at Oxford in 1555, "Latimer leaneth to Cranmer, Cranmer leaneth to Ridley, and Ridley to the singularity of his own wit." Clark, *Eucharistic Sacrifice and the Reformation*, 164.

and authorities of doctors."[19] Ridley denied any objective presence of Christ at the altar by virtue of consecration holding that the "spiritual communication of the flesh of Christ is not received in the Supper only, but also at other times, by hearing the gospel and by faith."[20] Although Van den Brink deduces that Peter Martyr first brought Ratramn's work to Ridley's attention, Dugmore thinks the deduction is arbitrary because the first translation of Ratramn's work appeared in 1548 just after Peter Martyr's arrival in England on December 20, 1547. However, Ratramn's work was known beforehand to Stephen Gardiner and perhaps Cuthbert Trunstall.[21] Ridley joined the attack with Cranmer[22] against transubstantiation in the House of Lords in December 1548.[23] C.C. Richardson, in his work *Zwingli and Cranmer on the Eucharist*, denies Cranmer's view is Calvinistic "dynamic receptionism" but Zwinglian because Cranmer believed that "the gift of which the elements are seals and pledges is not participation in the substance of the Body of Christ (as for Calvin), but sharing in the virtue of the Passion by faith, which is a somewhat different thing."[24] Ridley ends his catena of fathers in his Determination at Cambridge in June 1549 and his Disputation at Oxford months later with quotations from "Bertram," a misnomer for Ratramn.[25] In reaction, Paul IV placed it on the Index in 1559.[26]

---

19. C.W. Dugmore, review of J.N. Bakhuizen van den Brink's *Ratramnus: De Corpore et Sanguine Domini: texte etabli d'apres les manuscrits et notice bibliographique*. (Amsterdam: North-Holland Publishing Company, 1954), *Journal of Ecclesiastical History* (April 1956) 7:83.

20. Clark, *Eucharistic Sacrifice and the Reformation*, 165.

21. Dugmore, *Ratramnus: De Corpore et Sanguine Domini*, 7:84

22. C.C. Richardson, *Zwingli and Cranmer on the Eucharist* (Evanston, Ill.: 1949), 22, 48. Clark, *Eucharistic Sacrifice and the Reformation*, 164.

23. Clark, *Eucharistic Sacrifice and the Reformation*, 165; cf. Gasquet and Bishop, *Edward VI and the Book of Common Prayer*, chapter X.

24. Richardson, *Zwingli and Cranmer*, 22, 48. Clark, *Eucharistic Sacrifice and the Reformation*, 164.

25. Ridley, *A Brief Declaration of the Lord's Supper*, 197-99 (Appendix 1)

26. Dugmore, *Ratramnus: De Corpore et Sanguine Domini*, 7:84; Thomas M. Parker, review of *Ratramnus: De Corpero et Sanguine Domini: Texte original*

Several significant works appeared in the last century on Ratramn. In 1903, August Naegle published his work *Ratramn und die heilige Eucharisti*, wherein he argued that Ratramn held to the real presence in the elements.[27] In 1912, Raoul Heurtevent concluded with Naegle that Ratramn held to the real presence.[28] Heurtevent focused, however, on the issue of Ratramn's authenticity: "first, there was condemned at Vercelli a book on the Eucharist which they then believed to be from the hand of John the Scot. This has never been the object of the least doubt. Secondly, Ratramn is certainly the author of *De Corpore* which is attributed to him. Finally, the third certain fact is that the book condemned at Vercelli is Ratramn's book."[29] In 1926, another historian, Josef Geiselmann, argued in *Die Eucharistielehre der Vorschoolastik* that despite "realist terminology Ratramn actually limited the realism of the Eucharist to that of a symbolic entity."[30] Therefore, both Aquinas and Geiselmann see Ratramn as, more or less, in the Zwinglian fold while Moehler sees him in the Lutheran fold. Ratramn, of course, would have defined himself an Augustinian.

---

et notive bibliiogaphique. Edition renouvelee par J. N. Bakuizen van den Brink. (Amsterdam, London: North Holland Publishing Company, 1974), *Journal of Theological Studies*, n.s., 29:245–47 (April 1978), 246.

27. August Naegle, *Ratramnus und die heilige Eucharistie* (Wien: Veralg Von Mayer, 1903).

28. Raoul Heurtevent, *Durand de Troarn et les Origines de l'Heresie Berengarienne* (Paris: Beauchesne, 1912).

29. Heurtevent, *Durand de Troarn*, 277ff.

30. Josef Geiselmann, *Die Eucharistielehre der Vorschoolastik in Forshungen zur Christlichen Literatur-und Dogmengeschechte*, ed. by A. Ehrhard and J.P. Kirsch, (Paderborn: Druck und Verlag von Ferdinand Schoningh, 1926), XV, 195.

Chapter 8

CONCLUSION

Contrasts Between Radbert and Ratramn

Contrasts between Radbert and Ratramn include the extent of the appeal to the fathers and Scripture, the relation of the figure to reality, and the exact nature of the consecrated elements. Although Radbert promised replete patristic support, he appeals directly to only Gregory the Great. Ratramn, however, appeals to Ambrose, Augustine, Isidore, Jerome, and Fulegentius. Further, Ratramn's work is more replete with biblical support.[1] Ratramn sees an ongoing figure—"the sacraments have assumed their names."[2] Radbert swallows up the figure in the reality. Ratramn denies a bodily change, seeing rather a spiritual change. Radbert sees a real but non-visible transformation. Ratramn sees the elements as "spiritually made," thus having power as Christ's body and blood. Radbert sees the elements as actually the body and blood of Christ, although only faith can discern this. Ratramn distinguishes between Christ's crucified body and the spiritual presence of that

---

1. Bromiley, *Historical Theology: An Introduction*, 162.

2. "Ratramnus of Corbie: Christ's Body and Blood," *Library of Christian Classics*, vol. 9 (31).

body in the elements.³ Radbert parallels the deity and humanity of Christ in the incarnation and then claims an analogous parallel between the elements and Christ's historical body.⁴

WHY RADBERT'S VIEW GAINED THE ASCENDANCY UNTIL THE REFORMATION

Tragically, Radbert's view gained the ascendency, perhaps for four reasons. First, Radbert's view eliminated the crasser implications of the Capharnaitic sect.⁵ Second, Berengarius supported the resistance to an offensive literalism in Radbert.⁶ Third, Radbert's work, designed to be read to the unlettered faithful, circulated more widely among the lay folk while Ratramn's work circulated largely in scholarly circles.⁷ And fourth, with Ratramn's condemnation in 1058, his work would "simmer under veil" until its emergence under the Swiss and Anglican reformers.⁸

THE EXEGETICAL CONTINENTAL DIVIDE

The crossroads at which Radbert and Ratramn diverge is the interpretation of the words of the institution, "this is my body" (Matt. 26:27; Mark 14:23; Luke 22:17, 19; cf. 1 Cor. 11:26).⁹ If it is to be

    3. "Ratramnus of Corbie," LCC, vol. 9 (69).

    4. Bromiley quips that this distinction actually applies better for Radbert than Ratramn. Bromiley, *Historical Theology: An Introduction*, 165.

    5. Bromiley, *Historical Theology: An Introduction*, 165.

    6. Bromiley, *Historical Theology: An Introduction*, 165.

    7. But Bishop of Haymo of Halberstadt, for example, argued in the ninth century for outright transubstantiation: "the invisible priest, through his secret power, transforms his visible creatures into the substance of his flesh and blood. But although the nature of the substances has completely been turned into the body and blood of Christ, in the miracle of partaking, the taste and appearance of this body and blood remain those of bread and wine. Haymo, *De corp. et sang. Dom.* (PL 118:815–16).

    8. Bromiley, *Historical Theology: An Introduction*, 165.

    9. Augustine explains in In Evangelium Johannis tractatus 26, "therefore this is what it means to eat that food and drink that cup, namely, to remain

CONCLUSION

viewed as a figure of speech, then Ratramn is accurate; if it is to be viewed in a literal sense, then Radbert is correct. Intertwined with the crucial words of the institution is the bread of life discourse of John 6. In the same vein, if the bread of life is a figure, Ratramn is accurate; if literal, Radbert is correct. However, Christ resolved the divergence by explaining that the physical (sarx) does not profit, but the Spirit gives life—the word is spirit and life (John 6:63). In other words, the word is the agent of the life-imparting Spirit. Significantly, Ratramn quotes John 6:63 four times and concludes that the words of the institution convey literal truth via a rhetorical figure of speech. Christ also said "I am the door." Would Radbert have said that Christ was a piece of wood (sic)? God forbid.

---

in Christ and have Him remain in you. And thus he who does not remain in Christ and in whom Christ does not remain certainly does not eat the flesh of Christ spiritually or drink His blood." In *Evangelium Johannis tractatus* 88. "Brethren, you see the heavenly bread; eat it with your spiritual mouth." In *Evangelium Johannis tractatus* 90.

APPENDIX

A Comparison of Radbert's and Ratramn's Use of Supporting Scripture

A. *Radbert's Biblical Base—Proof Texts in the LC*[1]*C edition of* The Lord's Body and Blood

1. Ps. 115:3 (113:11, Vulgate)—the Creator willed that the elements be "in a mystery," that is, the true flesh and true blood of Christ.

2. John 6:51—"my flesh for the life of the world" refers to the Lord's Supper. John 1:14—indeed, the Word was made flesh, and this flesh becomes the food in the mystery of the sacrament.

4. Lev. 22:14—eating "the holy things" requires that the holiness of the one partaking, lest they "profane the holy things" of the children of Israel which they offer to the Lord.

5. Prov. 23:1—as one is advised to pay careful attention to what is placed at the table of a powerful man, so the communicant at the Lord's table must pay careful attention because he sits with one more powerful than the one alluded to in Proverbs.

---

1. *LCC Library of Christian Classics*

APPENDIX

6. Ps. 84:2 (83:3, Vulgate)—as the "heart" and "flesh" cry out to the living God, so the bodily senses should eagerly exult in the sacrament.

7. Rom. 6:9—although the flesh and blood of the Lamb is daily consumed by the faithful, the Lamb remains alive and whole, for he does not die.

8. Lev. 22:16—the Lord who said "I am the Lord who sanctifies them" provides a way for the reborn in Christ to have their iniquities born by Christ.

9. 2 Cor. 5:7—by walking by faith and not by sight, the divine power teaches the souls of believers about invisible things.

10. Rom. 1:17—the just should live by faith in the mysteries, that is, of the sacraments.

11. Rom. 8:9—those who partake of the sacrament participate in the common operation of the Holy Spirit, who animates the body of Christ, the church, to be one.

12. 1 Cor. 3:7—God gives the increase, that is, through the sacrament we may be prepared for things immortal and eternal.

13. Ezek. 1:21—the Spirit of life was in the wheels.

14. Rev. 2:7—the one who has ears to hear should hear what the Spirit says.

15. John 6:55–56—Christ said that his flesh is truly food, and his blood is truly drink.

16. John 6:51—the one who eats Christ's flesh and drinks his blood abides in Him and He in the communicant.

17. John 6:53—the condition of eternal life is consumption of Christ's body and blood.

18. Heb. 1:3—not every figure is a shadow or a falsity, because Christ is called the "figure of" God's substance.

19. Luke 22:19—the Lord said, "this is my body.

A COMPARISON OF RADBERT'S AND RATRAMN'S USE OF SUPPORTING

20. 1 Cor. 10:3—as our fathers "ate the same spiritual food and all drank the same spiritual drink," so communicants partake of the body and blood of the Lord.
21. Ps. 78:25 (77:25 Vulgate)—Christ was at an earlier time prefigured to believers, including in the figure "angels' food."
22. John 6:54–55—the one who eats and drinks the body of Christ has eternal life.
23. John 6:49—the fathers ate manna but died in the wilderness because they ate carnally, but those who partake of the sacrament spiritually enjoy eternal life.
24. 1 Cor. 11:29—those who partake unworthily receive a judgment upon themselves.
25. 1 Cor. 11:28—a communicant should first test himself before partaking.
26. Ps. 59:8 (58:9 Vulgate)—God scoffs at the scoffers, including at the unbelieving Jew who sought to mock the elements of the Eucharist.
27. Gal. 6:7—God will make sure those who mock will themselves reap what they sow, as in the case of the mocking Jew.
28. Mark 4:24—the measure whereby one measures will be their own measure, also as in the case of the mocking Jew.
29. Luke 2:25—to the faithless the Word is danger and destruction, but to the faithful the Word is life and exaltation.

B. Ratramn's Biblical Base—Proof Texts in the LC²C edition of Christ's Body and Blood

1. 1 Cor. 1:10—Paul urges that there be no schism rending the church.
2. Luke 11:3—the "bread" in the Lord's Prayer is a figure.

---

2. *LCC Library of Christian Classics*

APPENDIX

3. John 6:41—Christ's self-designation of "living bread" is a figure.
4. John 15:5—the "vine" and "branches" are figures.
5. Heb. 11:1—if the elements were in actuality the historical body of Jesus, faith would not operate, being replaced by sight; but faith is the "evidence of things not appearing."
6. Matt. 26:26—Christ said "take and eat: this is my body."
7. Matt. 26:28; Mark 14:24—Christ also said "take and drink: this is the blood of the New Testament which shall be shed for you."
8. Rom. 6:11, 13—Ratramn draws an analogy with baptism, which is "not undeservedly," according to him, called the "fountain of life."
9. 1 Cor. 10:1–4—the fathers were baptized into Christ "in the cloud and in the sea."
10. Ps. 78:25—in both the manna and the elements Christ is meant.
11. Luke 22:19ff.—Christ said, "this is the cup, the New Testament, in my blood, which shall be shed for you."
12. John 6:53—the condition of having life is to eat the flesh of the Son of Man, and drink his blood.
13. John 6:52—Ratramn holds that to literally eat and drink the body would have been a crime.
14. John 6:61ff.—since Christ would ascend, he intended the figures to communicate the mystery of the Eucharist.
15. John 6:63—the flesh is of no avail, so that if one partakes without faith, one only imbibes physically, not spiritually.
16. John 6:66—taking Christ's words literally involves a crime.
17. 1 Pet. 2:21—Christ suffered, leaving an example, but he does not say that he suffers in his own person daily. Rather the mystery is daily represented before believers.

18. Prov. 23:1—the one sitting at the table of the mighty should be careful how he acts.
19. Heb. 7:26-28—Christ, the great High Priest, died once for all.
20. Matt. 26:27; Mark 14:23; Luke 22:17, 19—the words of institution.
21. John 6:50-51—the one who partakes of Christ, the living bread Which came down from heaven, shall never die.
22. Matt. 26:26—Christ proclaimed, "this is my body."
23. Luke 22:19—Luke also records Christ's words, "this is my body."
24. Ps. 34:8 (39:9 Vulgate)—we are enjoined to taste and see that the Lord is good.
25. 1 Cor. 10:3-4—the fathers ate spiritual food and ate spiritual drink.
26. Ps. 104:12ff.—food strengthens and wine gladdens the heart, but "that" food and "that" drink of 1 Cor. 10:3-4 refers to the body of Christ, the body of the divine Spirit.
27. John 6:55—Christ explained that his flesh and blood are indeed food and drink.
28. John 19:34—Jerome distinguishes between the spiritual food and drink of Christ's body and the historical body, pierced by a spear.
29. Rom. 6:9—Christ who died and rose again is eternal and therefore incapable of suffering.
30. Rom. 8:9—only the one who has the Spirit of Christ belongs to him.
31. John 6:63 (4X)—the flesh is of no avail, but the spirit gives life—the words that Christ spoke are spirit and life.
32. Luke 24:39—Christ told the disciples after the resurrection to touch and see that a spirit does not have flesh and bones.

APPENDIX

33. Acts 20:28—Fulgentius explains that the blood of God was shed in a single sacrifice offered, revealed to sight.
34. Is. 7:9—faith requires instruction, and unless one believes, they will not understand.
35. 1 Cor. 12:27—believers are members of Christ's body, who partaking of one bread, are one in Christ.
36. 1 Cor. 10:17—we who are many, are one bread, one body in Christ.
37. Luke 22:19—Christ said do this in remembrance of me.
38. 1 Cor. 11:26 — eating and drinking in the Lord's Supper is proclamation of the Lord's death until he comes again.
39. John 6:63 — the Spirit gives life while the flesh is of no avail.

BIBLIOGRAPHY

Aherne, C.M. *New Catholic Encyclopedia.* Washington, D.C.: Catholic University of America, 1967.

Aulen, Gustaf. *Eucharist and Sacrifice.* Translated by Eric H. Wahlstrom. Philadelphia: Muhlenberg Press, 1958.

Barbet, Jeanne, ed. Iohannis Scoti Eriugenae Expositiones in Ierarchiam coelestem. *Corpus Christianorum, Continuatio Medievalis XXI.* Turnhout: Brepols, 1975.

Bonano, S. "The Divine Maternity and the Eucharistic Body and the Doctrine of Paschasius Radbertus," *EphemMar,* 1, 1951.

Bouhot Jean-Paul. *Ratramne de Corbie: Histoire letteraire et controverses doctrinales.* Paris, 1976.

Bromiley, Geoffrey W. *Historical Theology: An Introduction.* Grand Rapids: Wm. B. Eerdmans, 1978.

Chemnitz, Martin. *The Lord's Supper.* Translated by J.A.O. Preus, reprint ed., *De coena Domoni, 1590* St. Louis: Concordia Publishing House, 1979.

Clark, Francis. *Eucharistic Sacrifice and the Reformation.* Westminster, MD.: The Newman Press, 1960.

Colish, Marcia L. "Carolingian Debates over Nihil and Tenebrae: A Study in Theological Method," *Speculum* 59, 1984.

Dolger, F.J. *Der helige Tisch in den antiken Religionen und im Christentum.* Munster I. W., 2d ed., 1928

Fahey, John. *The Eucharistic Teaching of Ratramn of Corbie.* Mundelein, Ill.: Saint Mary of the Lake Seminary, 1951.

Gasquet, Aiden Cardinal and Edmund Bishop. *Edward VI and the Book of Common Prayer.* 1928.

Geiselmann, Josef. *Die Eucharistielehre der Vorschoolastik in Forshungen zur Christlichen Literatur-und Dogmengeschechte.* Edited by A. Ehrhard and J.P. Kirsch. Paderborn: Druck und Verlag von Ferdinand Schoningh, 1926.

Gonzalez, Julio L. *A History of Christian Thought: From Augustine to the Eve of the Reformation* vol. 2. Nashville: Abingdon, 1971.

Gore, Charles. *The Body of Christ: An Inquiry into the Institution and Doctrine of Holy Communion.* London: John Murray, 1901.

BIBLIOGRAPHY

Guitmond, *De corporis et sanguinis Christi vertitate in Eucharistia*, 1415.

Haugh, Richard Stanley. "The Byzantine-Carolingian Triadological Controversy with a View toward its Appeal to Tradition and the Fathers." PhD diss., Fordham University, 1973.

Heurtevent, Raoul. *Durand de Troarn et les Origines de l'Heresie Berengarienne.* Paris: Beauchesne, 1912.

Hincmar, De div. Lot. et Tet. 12, n.d.

Irenaeus, *Adversus haereses*, n.d.

Jasper, R.C.D. and G.J. Cuming, *Prayers of the Eucharist: Early and Reformed.* New York: Oxford University Press, 1980.

Lambot, C., ed. *De corpore et sanguine domini. OEuvres theologique et grammaticales de Godescalc d'Orbais Spicilegium sacrum lovaniense.* Louvain, 1945.

Lambot, D.C. *Liber de anima ad Odonem Bellovacensem, Analecta mediaevalia Namurcensia.* Namur, 1951.

Macdonald, A.J. *Berengar and the Reform of Sacramental Doctrine.* London: Longmans, Green and Co., 1930.

Macy, Gary. *The Theologies of the Eucharist in the Early Scholastic Period: A Study of the Salvific Function of the Sacrament according to the Theologians c. 1080–c. 1220.* Oxford: Clarendon Press, 1984.

Migne, J.P., ed. *Patrologia Latina.* Paris 1878–90.

Moehler, John. *Symbolism, or Exposition of the Doctrinal Differences between Catholics and Protestants.* Translated by James B. Robertson. 3rd ed. New York: The Catholic Publishing, 1894.

Naegle, August. *Ratramnus und die heilige Eucharistie.* Wien: Veralg Von Mayer, 1903.

Packer, J.I. *Introduction: Lambeth, 1958, in Eucharistic Sacrifice: The Addresses Given at the Oxford Conference of Evangelical Churchmen.* London: Church Book Room Press, 1962.

Pohle, J. CE 11.518.

Radbertus, *De partu Virg.* 1 (PL, 120:1368–69).

Ratramn, "Ratramnus of Corbie: Christ's Body and Blood," *Library of Christian Classics*, vol. 9.

Ratramnus, *De corp et sang.* Dom. 5 ed. J.N.B. van den Brink. Amsterdam: Noord-Hollandse Uitgervers Mig., 1954.

Richardson, C.C. *Zwingli and Cramner on the Eucharist.* Evanston, Ill.: 1949.

Ridley, Nicholas. *A Brief Declaration of the Lord's Supper.* Edited by H.C.G. Moule (reprint ed., New York: Thomas Whittaker, 1895.

Ripberger, Albert, ed. *Der Pseudo-Hieronymus-Brief IX "Cogitis me." Ein erster marianischer Traktat des Mittelalters von Paschasius Radbert.* Freiburg, Switzerland, 1962.

Schweitzer, Albert. *The Lord's Supper in Relationship to the Life of Jesus and the History of the Early Church.* Macon, Ga.: Mercer University, 1982.

Stone, Darwell. *A History of the Doctrine of the Holy Eucharist.* New York: Longmans, Green, and Co., 1909.

BIBLIOGRAPHY OF SUPPORTING SCRIPTURE

Vermigli, Peter Martyr. *The Discourse of Peter Martyr upon the Sacrament of the Lord's Supper.* University Microfilms, Ann Arbor, MI: University Microfilm, 1550. Photostat.

Wilmart, A. *Corbie, Dictionnaire d'Archeologie Chretienne et de Liturgie*[1]

---

1. House, H. W. (2014). Radbertus and Ratramnus—Their Controversy Regarding the Eucharist. In *Radbertus vs. Ratramnus: Their Controversy as to the Nature of the Eucharistic Elements.* Charleston, SC: George J. Gatgounis.

www.ingramcontent.com/pod-product-compliance
Lightning Source LLC
Chambersburg PA
CBHW070100100426
42743CB00012B/2606